Corporate Strategy
Portfolio Models

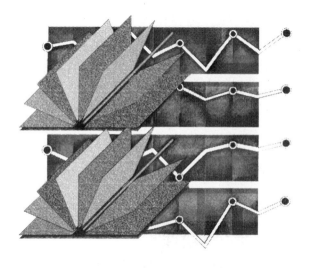

Corporate Strategy
Portfolio Models

ELI SEGEV
Tel Aviv University

International Thomson Publishing / boyd & fraser

London • Bonn • Boston • Madrid • Melbourne • Mexico City • New York • Paris • Singapore
Tokyo • Toronto • Albany, NY • Belmont, CA • Cincinnati, OH • Detroit, MI

Corporate Strategy:
Portfolio Models

International Thomson Publishing
    Commissioning Editor: Diane M. Van Bakel
    Editorial Assistant: Samantha Brown
boyd & fraser
    Senior Acquisitions Editor: DeVilla Williams

Made in Logotechnics C.P.C. Ltd., Sheffield
    Project Management: Sandra M. Potestà
    Production: Hans-Dieter Rauschner + Team
    Artistic Direction: Stefano E. Potestà
    Cover Illustration: William Smith

First printed 1995

International Thomson Publishing   boyd & fraser
Berkshire House   One Corporate Place
168–173 High Holborn   Ferncroft Village
London WC1V 7AA   Danvers, MA 01923

ISBN (ITP UK)   1-850-32133-7
ISBN (boyd & fraser)   0-87709-929-4

British Library Cataloguing-in-Publication Data
A catalogue record for this book is available from the British Library

Library of Congress Cataloging-in-Publication Data
A catalog record for this book is available from the Library of Congress

"The wretched and lean cows ate the seven sleek and fat cows."

Genesis, 40,4.

Contents

Foreword

The boyd & fraser Series in Decision Making and Operations Management comprises a set of books to help people at all levels, from undergraduates to graduates to executive managers. The focus is on understanding how to make choices, be they at the operational, managerial, or strategic level. The volumes in the series cover a wide range, from the practical to the the theoretical. The series covers material typically taught in the classic disciplines of decision making, quantitative methods, production, productivity and operations management typically taught in business schools and in industrial engineering. The authors are leaders in their fields.

The present two-volume set focuses on strategic decision making. This subject has been approached from both a behavioral and a quantitative point of view. At one extreme are people who believe that only the human aspects are important, whereas at the other extreme the financial numbers are over-riding. The truth is probably in between, behaviorists have to pay attention to the numbers and the finance people must deal with the human implications of strategy making. In this volume, the focus is on the use of models to help decision makers understand the nature of the strategic problem. Although based on numbers (very few of which are financial), the output is visual and designed to give the decision maker the ability to see the implications of proposed changes. The results form the basis for making judgement.

The present two-volume set is very practical. It is concerned with decisions that managers of firms with multiple business units face over and over. Does my present set of strategies make sense for the organisation as a whole? Are there ways that I can change my corporate strategy or the detailed strategies for individual units to improve the performance of the entire enterprise? Are there acquisitions that I need to make? Should I divest one or more of my units? These decisions are at the heart of the corporate strategy problem. The questions have engaged scholars for many years.

Eli Segev is a Harvard DBA with over 20 years of experience in corporate planning. In this book he brings together the thinking of the leading experts in the field. The basic approach to dealing with multiple business units is to consider the units as a portfolio, much like a stock investment portfolio. Experts have created relatively simple matrices (one as small as 2×2, others somewhat larger) on which to characterize each business unit. Segev recognizes that, while there are many such matrix portfolio methods available, each approach is designed to work best under specific situations and has its own advantages and shortcomings. He deals with seven of the most popular models and additionally offers the reader the opportunity to create their own portfolio model.

The first volume, *Corporate Strategy: Portfolio Models*, is directed at understanding the portfolio concept and each of the seven models that deal with it. It presents the underlying ideas in simple, direct terms. It tells you which situations are best for each model. It allows you to make an intelligent choice depending on your own situation. It covers not only the well-known Boston Consulting Group matrix with its Stars and Dogs, and the GE/McKinsey model, but models that bring into consideration such additional factors as risk and return.

The second volume, *Navigating by COMPASS*, allows you to apply each of these models to your own situation. *Navigating by COMPASS* is a practice orientated book. Accompanied by a DOS disk, it lets you put each of the models up on your own IBM-compatible computer and study the implications of both your present strategy and future strategies. It is a visual, hands-on approach that requires almost no computer expertise beyond turning the machine on and off and following instructions.

The two volumes complement one another. They can be used alone or in combination. Each will give you a superb understanding of the nature of the corporate strategy decision problem. Each will help you make important decisions.

Paul Gray
Series Editor
Claremont, California

Preface

What is in this book?

Corporations can be viewed as arrays of different business units, frequently supplying many product lines to multiple markets. Matrix portfolio analysis is a technique for displaying a multi-business-unit firm as a 'portfolio' of businesses, charting or categorizing the different businesses, and determining the implications for the corporation's top management. Several portfolio analysis techniques have been developed over the past 25 years. The best known and most widely used are the Boston Consulting Group (BCG) grid, the General Electric/McKinsey (GE/McKinsey) matrix and the Shell/Directional Policy Matrix (Shell/DPM).

Though the different portfolio techniques are planning tools to be used as aids in business evaluation and in the making of corporate strategy, they each stress different planning elements, be it cash flow planning, investment allocation, internal deployment of funds, risk taking, or profit planning. This book integrates the use of seven different approaches to corporate portfolio analysis.

It provides a multi-model approach to corporate portfolio analysis which offers managers the benefits of all the important techniques, without subjecting them to the limitations inherent in using any single one. Moreover, when different models are used interactively, a new and better tool for corporate strategy making emerges.

The contribution of this book

Throughout the book you will learn about how to employ the different portfolio matrices presented. We have also tried to show you that different portfolio matrices can be used for various purposes.

Choose a portfolio model

The models presented in this book are based on different assumptions, different goal functions, and different dimensions. Any one may be usefully applied in examining corporate strategy.

Identify corporate strategy

By using the variety of portfolio models discussed here, managers can deepen their understanding of current corporate strategy.

Seek strategic alternatives

Theoretically, the existence of multiple business units within a corporation allows for endless strategic combinations and permutations. In practice, most alternative mixes are not viable. On the basis of the normative prescriptions offered by the various models, the book enables managers to focus on a manageable number of possible strategic alternative mixes of strategic business units (SBUs), each being consistent with corporate strategy.

Fine-tune strategy with 'What if'

When seeking different points of view, and analyzing different possible future scenarios, managers can use the different models to change, reevaluate and fine-tune alternative strategies.

This volume is not a textbook on strategy and policy. However, when you read it, you will know a lot about the practicalities of corporate-level strategies and something about business-level strategies. You will be introduced to the main concepts and variables, the important schools of analysis, the theories and the findings. But the most important thing this book teaches you is how to use this knowledge systematically. You will learn how to:

1. Identify past and current corporate strategies;

2. Analyze the potentials and limitations of the corporation and its SBUs relative to its competitors;

3. Recognize imbalances in the portfolio;

4. Identify areas for development, acquisition and divestment;

5. Formulate a preferred corporate strategy;

6. Plan to implement the preferred strategy over time.

The approach presented here is comprehensive and integrative, allowing you to deal with seven different portfolio models in detail.

Limitations of this book

We scarcely use financial information. Just as Alice, before going down into Wonderland, doubted the value of books without dialogue or pictures, a manager may doubt the value of a book on strategy that does not consider financial data. To some readers, our use of qualitative rather than quantitative data may seem a little vague and imprecise. Well, that is the way strategies are determined. At the beginning of every elaborate and detailed five-year plan, complete with *pro forma* yearly balance sheets and income statements, there is a subjective strategy. Since we focus on corporate strategy making, the result is strategy rather than detailed five-year *pro forma* financial statements.

We relate to some important aspects of business unit strategies, as well as some functional strategies, but do not elaborate. This book is intended for managers involved in corporate-level strategy making. It takes the CEO's point of view. Those CEOs who also assume responsibility for specific functional strategy making in areas such as finance, marketing, production, R&D, human resources, or information systems, will find it insufficient for their needs in the functional area and are advised to complement it with books that focus on the strategies of the specific functional areas.

The book does not deal with particular business-level strategy typologies. If you are interested in learning more about business-level strategy, you might read *Business SUCCESS*, by Eli Segev and Paul Gray.

Most importantly, remember that we present a diagnostic tool at the manager's disposal. It provides direction but not direct solutions. Do not expect analysis to dictate which specific SBU a corporation should target for development or acquisition. By using the various models, managers will learn to recognize when the corporate portfolio is unbalanced. Furthermore, they will be able to discern the qualities desirable in a candidate for acquisition or development to rectify the imbalance. Should the manager have a specific SBU in mind, any or all of the models may be used to check the fit between the SBU and the needs of the portfolio and corporate strategy.

In brief, the first chapter provides an overview and introduces key concepts in corporate strategy and the use of matrix portfolio analysis tools. The following seven chapters have a standard format. Each chapter introduces one of the seven matrix portfolio analysis approaches. We describe each approach and point out its strengths and weaknesses, uses and misuses. In Chapter 9, we offer readers/users the opportunity to create a custom-made matrix portfolio analysis approach that suits the needs of their corporation.

For whom is this book intended?

The book is aimed at three markets:

1. Senior executives responsible for running corporations, as well as managers of business units that are part of larger corporations.

2. MBA students in courses on business policy. This book would supplement the classic texts used in most such courses. It allows students to understand the implications of their attempts to devise corporate strategy, as well as the interrelationships between the business units' strategies and corporate strategy.

3. Executives enrolled in Executive MBA Programs and Advanced Management Programs, for whom corporate strategy is not an abstract matter but a serious day-to-day concern. We believe that very few existing texts are aimed at this population, and that it represents an important market segment.

The book is based on the idea that managers should identify and evaluate their corporate strategy personally. It is oriented toward managers, not only to their staff members. It developed out of the firm belief that though they may be assisted by staff and/or outside consultants, top managers cannot subcontract or delegate corporate strategy downwards.

This book is comprehensive and complete. Readers wishing to pursue portfolio models further, and those interested in a practical analysis support system are referred to Segev, E., *Navigating by COMPASS: Corporate Matrix Portfolio Analysis Support System.*

Acknowledgments

The writing of this book started in Claremont, California and continued in Tel-Aviv, Israel. The project of writing a book so comprehensive cannot be accomplished in a reasonable length of time without the help of graduate students, for which I am extremely grateful. Specifically, at the Faculty of Management, Tel Aviv University, I am indebted to Dr. Tamar Almor Ellemers, Wendy Fingold, Berl Glass, Shai Farkash, Karen Fainman, Adi Bildner, Lori Erlich, and Erez Perlmuter; and at The Claremont Graduate School to James E. Rhodes, Ben Mortagy, and Mike (Jungki) Min.

I am grateful for the advice and insight provided by many practicing managers and MBA students who were exposed to early drafts as they were developed. Special thanks are due to my friend and colleague Professor Igal Ayal for his invaluable review and contributions, to Gerda Kessler for her copyediting, and to Hanna Vilozny for her meticulous typing and administrative help.

Eli Segev
Tel-Aviv, Israel

1

Corporate strategy and portfolio models

Corporate strategy defined

Strategy again

'Strategy' has been borrowed from the military, 'Policy' from politics. Their use in business is the same. The concept of business strategy has evolved over time, although the basic idea has not changed. For example, a 1962 definition stated that strategy is 'the determination of the basic long-term goals and objectives of an enterprise, and the adoption of course of action and the allocation of resources necessary for carrying out these goals[1].' That is, strategy is the alignment of goals and courses of action of an organization.

Strategy is created at the topmost level of an organization. This level, intentionally or not, sets the organization's goals and decides on its investments and the deployment of its resources. Although many other forces

1

have an impact on strategy, it is the mandate of top management to make strategy. Any ongoing business has a strategy, whether it thinks so or not. Even if the strategy is undocumented, informal, or unplanned, and even if the business is unaware of, unconscious of, or flatly denies it, a strategy exists. A strategy is created because a working organization cannot be totally flexible and turn around instantly. Location, premises, facilities, technology, employees, product lines, target market, supply and distribution channels, reputation, standards, and procedures, to name a few, are chosen, created, and adhered to for various lengths of time. The decisions and investments made in the past create organizational inertia and momentum.

Organizational inertia and momentum change over time. Few business organizations are totally rigid from start-up to divestment. Most organizations modify and change, some are even revolutionized. However, these are not daily changes. Over time, organizational inertia and momentum create a unique business pattern of investments and activities. The essence of this pattern may be identified, analyzed and modified. This pattern has a name: strategy. Thus, even though it may be unplanned, unintentional, nondeliberate, or even misdirected, strategy exists. It exists because most managerial decisions are consistent and logical. When defined and adopted consciously, a formal strategy can become a set of guidelines for future activities.

Successful or not, strategy definition is made by top management. In the literature, some authors divide an orderly, formal corporate planning process into hierarchies of aims, goals, objectives, policies, strategies, and programs. In this book, for clarity and manageability, we will divide strategy making into phases, but will treat it as a single concept.

The hierarchy of strategies: Corporate, business unit, and functional

Although strategy is a comprehensive concept, it is sometimes applied to different kinds and levels of organizations, organizational activities, or geographic regions. Thus, people talk about divisional strategy, export strategy, West Coast strategy, or departmental strategy. One categorization, used in this book, follows the way businesses organize and separate strategy into:

- Corporate strategy (which includes many business units),

- Business-level strategy (one business unit),

- Functional strategy (functions such as finance, information systems, marketing).

The definitions of business unit and business strategy are intertwined. A business unit is 'the level in the organization at which the responsibility for the formulation of a multifunctional strategy for a single industry or product–market arena is determined'[2] whereas a business strategy is the competitive weapons used to give a business unit its distinctive competence within its industry.[3] Thus, business strategy is one level above functional strategies. In a well-run firm, functional strategies are included in the business unit strategy. Conversely, the functional strategies are guided, coordinated, and directed by the business unit's strategy. Ideally, functional strategies comprise together a consistent and comprehensive business unit strategy.

Many organizations are single business units, and thus their business unit strategy is their highest level of strategy. On the other hand, many large organizations are corporations composed of multi-industry or multi-product–market units. For these firms, corporate-level strategy involves the selection of product markets or industries and allocation of resources among them.[4] This book deals with corporate strategy.

Example:

In 1981, the Coca-Cola Company issued a pamphlet called '*Strategy for the 80s*'. According to this statement, Coca-Cola's corporate-level strategy stated that packaged consumer goods and consumer services are the businesses that Coca-Cola prefers. The corporate aim was to maintain or improve position in current businesses, increasing earnings per share annually. In addition Coca-Cola aimed to increase return on assets, while entering new businesses that were felt to have growth potential. The various business strategies were defined for each business unit. For example, in soft drinks Coca-Cola would follow a stability strategy, working to maintain its leadership position. In foods as well, the strategy was stability, working to maintain market share in frozen fruit juices, coffee, and so on. In wine, on the other hand, a concentrated strategy was to be followed, with the company trying to match its growth to the growth of the wine industry. A typical functional-level strategy would be the decision to use aseptic packaging for preservatives or refrigeration for the HiC fruit drink.[5]

Corporate strategy

Corporations are multi-industry or multi-product–market units, that is, multi-unit business concerns. Corporations do not compete directly in the market place, they do it through their business units. True, when two or more technology-focused corporations are largely identified with relatively many common products/markets (as in the automotive or the computer industries) we tend to view these total corporations in direct competition. Even in these cases, while many business units of one corporation may compete with those of the other corporation, each corporation has unique business units, products and markets, outside the domain of its 'competitor'. For a diversified corporation, on the other hand, it is usually impossible to point out one major competitor. It has many different competitors in its various product–markets.

A corporation may compete with other businesses on the purchase/ acquisition/takeover of a firm, or on the introduction of new start-ups. A corporation may also cooperate with other businesses forming joint ventures. However, the battle for the final consumer is the responsibility of the business unit. The essence of corporate strategy is its mix and composition of business units. Corporate strategy encompasses its business philosophy and ideology, including a basic set of guidelines regarding its businesses. These guidelines may take into consideration industries and technologies, products and services, raw materials and employees' skills, countries and geographical locations, markets and customers, qualities and prices, margins and value-added, profits and cash flows, volumes and sizes, governmental regulations and export opportunities, or any operationalization of the corporate vision. So, the guidelines are made and used to maintain a rationale for the specific mix of business units composing the corporation. Next, these guidelines are followed by the top management of the corporation in acquiring and starting up new business units; in divesting existing business units; and in transferring resources among business units.

Corporate's business units do not have to be in the same industries and markets, employing similar technologies; however, successful corporate strategy generally limits the range of businesses in some way, in part to limit the specific expertise needed by top management. A good corporate strategy results in a business units mix whose total is greater than its parts: synergy. From an economic, and social, point of view there should be value added by the corporation. The added value may be the result of interrelationships among different business units (such as shared resources, outlets or transportation facilities, economies of scale, or R&D efforts), or the product of the corporation/business unit interrelationships (such as management, financial, or information system services). In other cases, each business unit can do better on its own.

Corporate guidelines are checked periodically and changed when external or internal conditions require strategic changes. No corporation is just composed of haphazard business units. Again, as we stated at the beginning of this chapter, discussing strategy in general, the corporate vision may be unprofitable or outdated, the guidelines may be wrongly made or implemented, and the corporation performance may be unsatisfactory. This is a POOR corporate strategy, not an UNstrategy.

Portfolio management

Origin of the concept

Portfolio is defined in Webster's dictionary as 'a hinged cover or flexible case for carrying loose papers, pictures, or pamphlets.' Applied to the business world, a portfolio is 'the securities held by an investor' or 'the commercial paper held by a financial house (as a bank).'

In a financial portfolio, individual investments are considered as components of a total investment plan. The expected return of a portfolio is a weighted average of the expected returns of its component securities, using relative values as weights. Its risk depends on the risk of its component securities, and also on the extent to which the returns of the different securities are products of the same events (that is, correlated). Thus, a portfolio can be used for risk reduction if its components are uncorrelated. An efficient portfolio has less risk than any other with comparable expected return and more return than any other with comparable risk.[6]

Portfolio applied to corporate

Applied to business organizations, portfolio analyses have their greatest applicability in developing strategy at the corporate level and in aiding in corporate review of business units, rather than in developing competitive strategy in individual industries. Portfolio analyses include different techniques for displaying a multi-business-unit firm as a 'portfolio' of businesses, charting or categorizing the different businesses in a firm's portfolio, and determining the implications for top management of the corporation. The firm can try to balance the portfolio in terms of its mix of developing and developed businesses and the internal consistency of cash generation and cash use, with major implications regarding the acquisition of business units, investment in start-ups, and divestment of existing business units. Thereby, it affects the relationships among established units by correcting resource allocation imbalances among groups, divisions, and business units.

Different levels in the organization may use the portfolio approach: product-line managers to balance their products; business units to balance their product lines or product–market units; and corporations, corporate groups, or corporate divisions to balance their business units. Thus this book is intended for the management of corporations, as well as corporate groups and divisions, that is, any manager whose responsibility encompasses more than a single business unit.

Purpose, use, objective, practice

A matrix analysis is a base point for corporate strategy making. It is used for identifying the current composition of business units. It facilitates micro and macro strategy making, at the corporate level. Focusing on a business unit, top management pinpoints the unit's location on a matrix which depicts its industry opportunities and its competitive competence. The corporate strategy makers need not, and cannot, be experts on the business unit technology, production, and marketing. These are the domains of business-unit-level detailed strategy making. At the corporate level, the business unit presentation on the matrix supplies the information and the tools for control, evaluation, deciding on general directions for the unit, and major resource allocation decisions.[7]

On the macro level, the strategy for the company as a whole must be evaluated. The multitude of business units in diverging industries (involving very different division managers, presidents, and staff specialists, all sometimes located in remote cities around the globe) fosters disconnected strategy making. The tendency is toward fragmented, *ad hoc* strategy making focusing mainly on current key issues and needs. This tendency is harnessed by the use of a portfolio matrix as a planning tool.

Strategy making is guided by a complete representation of the corporate mix of business units. Major key issues and problems, which relate to the company as a whole, guide strategy making. The current situation is acknowledged, understood and analyzed. As a by-product, a common language is established and a group consensus in regard to the meaning of the information in the model is reached. Searching for possible methods of achieving a better-balanced portfolio is initiated. The search is guided by the identified weaknesses of the current portfolio. Corporate staff are directed to investigate the market possibilities for acquiring, or selling, certain business units. Technology is reviewed in the search for opportunities, and the outlines of a possible future portfolio emerge. Specific decisions on resource allocation are the building blocks of a concrete plan for reaching the desired future portfolio.

There is no universal framework for portfolio analysis. Several portfolio techniques have been developed in the past 25 years. This book incorporates seven different approaches to corporate portfolio analysis. Though all the different portfolio techniques are planning tools to aid in evaluation and in the making of corporate strategy, they were developed, and are used, for different purposes. Major stated direct purposes of these techniques include designing optimal cash flows between business units, guidance in investment allocation decisions (hold, penetrate), and in resource allocation and internal deployment of funds. In practice, portfolio approaches are used also for creating a shared vocabulary and supplying corporate management with graphic tools which facilitate communication and sharing of judgments and assumptions; in separating important decisions from non-important ones; in helping to pinpoint information gaps. Furthermore, they are used to force management to think about the future; focus attention on the opportunities for new units and creative thinking; and even for *post hoc* justification of investment strategies; and also, as a by-product of business unit scrutiny, in improving the quality of business unit plans and explaining them to corporate management.

Conceptual foundations

Is it: 'Invest in the most profitable areas'?

Ever since its initial presentation the matrix portfolio approach has been under fire. The approach was incubated in the business sector and implemented by management consultants and industry before it had been duly investigated by scholars in the universities. Criticism of the approach will be presented later as part of the discussion of specific models. However, one question should be addressed here.

The matrix portfolio approach was suggested as a substitute for the much criticized return-on-investment criterion which was popular in the early 1960s. It was Wensley[8, 9] who raised the question of whether the matrix portfolio approach is no more than 'invest in the most profitable areas'. The answer to this is yes, but with one reservation. Profitability is the driving force, but since different planning horizons, cash-flow limitations, and acceptable risk levels may impose constraints on profitability, the approach is in reality 'invest in the most *viable* profitable areas'!

SBU definition

Common to all models for portfolio planning is the unit of analysis – the strategic business unit (SBU), sometimes termed strategic center or SBA.[10] All too often managers who wish to implement portfolio planning in their companies focus too much of their attention upon the question of choice of analytic technique and not enough upon the identification and definition of the strategic business units. This first step is the most critical. The accurate designation of SBUs is crucial to the quality of portfolio analysis.

With the above in mind we will attempt to provide definitions and criteria for classifying strategic business units. Seldom are all criteria fully satisfied, the process of SBU definition generally being an exercise in compromise.[11]

A strategic business unit is sometimes considered to be a natural business or a strategy center. It is an independent unit of strategy used by businesses for the purpose of resource allocation.

Various formal definitions of an SBU exist. A broader definition describes the SBU as an organizational body housing all functions that are necessary for the realization of the business mission in an independent manner.[12] Another definition with a marketing orientation describes the SBU as an 'operating unit which sells a distinct set of products to an identifiable group of customers with a well defined set of competitors.'[13]

For strategic planning purposes it may be necessary to redefine existing operational units, as in many instances they do not correspond to the definition of the SBU. Their division might cut across existing organizational structures of divisions, profit centers or cost centers, making their distinction indeed problematic. The corporate manager must consider whether the organizational unit:

- exists as an autonomous business and as such is an SBU,

- contains more than one SBU,

- makes up part of an SBU,

- serves as a functional activity for a number of SBUs.

In order to facilitate the process of SBU identification and definition, the following criteria are presented as guidelines for the corporate manager's consideration:[14, 15]

- **Strategic autonomy.**
  The SBU maintains strategic autonomy within the corporation. It should be able to pursue its own strategic mission independently of other SBUs.

- **External market.**
  The SBU has an external product market. An organizational unit which is predominantly an internal corporate supplier cannot be defined as an SBU.

- **Distinct customer set.**
  The SBU's set of customers is distinct and separate from other SBUs. Should two or more business units share the same customers it is most likely that they are parts of a single SBU.

- **Distinct competitor set.**
  An SBU possesses a single set of competitors. This competitor set defines the industry in which the SBU operates. Should the SBU compete against more than one distinct set of competitors it may actually be more than one SBU.

- **Impact of price change.**
  A price change in any product of the SBU necessitates a similar price change in all other products of the SBU. If other products remain unaffected by the price change it would suggest the existence of more than one SBU.

- **Impact of quality/style change.**
  A change in the quality or styling characteristics of an SBU product necessitates similar change in other of the SBU's products.

- **Product substitutability.**
  Products sold by the SBU are substitutable. If products sold by a business unit cannot be substituted for one another it can be assumed that they belong to different SBUs.

- **Impact of divestment or liquidation.**
  Should the selling or dropping of a product or product line affect the effectiveness of the marketing or selling of other products belonging to the SBU, it is fair to conclude that the business is indeed a single SBU. Should the effectiveness remain unchanged it can be assumed that the business unit is in fact more than one SBU.

- **Generation of real income.**
  An SBU generates real income rather than artificial 'monies' posted as transfer payments between divisions.

- **Senior manager.**
  An SBU is large enough to warrant the employment of a senior manager.

Some of the criteria may appear to overlap but each is significant. In practice, all the criteria are rarely fully satisfied. According to Hofer and Schendel,[16] while the development of focused product/market strategies requires that the number of product/market groups included in an SBU should be minimized, too strict adherence to SBU definition criteria would lead to overfragmentation and an unmanageable number of SBUs. As a result, it will often be necessary to cluster several different but related product/ market groups in a single SBU. Clustering decisions should take into account shared technologies and facilities and the similarity of markets and distribution systems. The end result should be a more meaningful number of SBUs which can be managed at the strategic level.[17]

Definition of Market/Industry

Implicit in the identification of the SBU is the definition of its market/industry. The delineation of the SBU's boundaries is to a large degree derived from the market it serves and the industry to which it belongs. In the list of criteria presented to guide SBU definition, the SBU's market is represented by its customer set and its industry by its competitor set.

The market stresses output aspects – the SBU's effort to satisfy customer needs and meet demand, while the industry stresses input aspects – the pursuance and utilization of resources by the SBU and its competitors. In portfolio planning the terms market and industry are used synonymously, the combination of the two representing a specific input–output relationship or the task environment in which the SBU operates. The stage of identifying the SBU's task environment is equally critical, as 'incorrect diagnosis of the market leads to erroneous view of market share and market growth and consequently, invalid strategic prescriptions.'[18]

Abell and Hammond[19] contend that a market is defined by choices along three dimensions:

1. Customer group – *who* is being satisfied.

2. Customer function – *what* need is being satisfied.

3. Technology – *how* the need is being satisfied.

The process of delineating the scope of an SBU's market should not proceed along one dimension at a time; it requires, rather, an interactive consideration of all dimensions simultaneously.[20]

According to Day,[21] choices along the dimensions will depend in part upon the approach to market definition employed. He describes two possible approaches – the 'bottom-up' and 'top-down' approaches. The bottom-up perspective is most often adopted by the product or market manager who is responsible for the performance of a specific SBU. The market is viewed in relation to the SBU's ability to satisfy shifting customer needs. This approach leads to a narrower, more tactical definition of the market.

The corporate planner or manager, who is responsible for the overall performance of the corporation, tends to define an SBU's market from a top-down perspective. Markets are observed in terms of the SBU's capacity to compete and to utilize corporate resources in order to establish a competitive advantage. This approach leads to a broader, more strategic view of the market.

Thus the scope of the market definition is a function of both purpose and approach. Should the objective be short-term performance evaluation, then the bottom-up approach is employed and the market is narrowly defined. If the purpose is the analysis of threats and opportunities, the top-down approach is adopted and the scope of the market is broader. Day suggests an integrated approach which exploits the differences in market definitions resulting from the two approaches.

Another approach to market/industry definition is provided by Porter.[22] He defines the market/industry in terms of five key structural forces:

- **Threat of entry.**
  The level of entrance barriers to an industry will affect the scope of market/industry definition. Low entrance barriers increase the threat of new competitors. These potential newcomers must be accounted for when the market is defined. High barriers tend to dissuade newcomers, thus narrowing the scope of the market/industry.

- **Substitutes.**
  The availability of substitutes is another factor which will circumscribe the breadth of the market definition. Substitutes are products which satisfy the same customer needs. Customers will opt for substitutes when the price of the product in question rises above an acceptable level; thus substitutes place price ceilings on the product. An abundance of substitute products will necessitate the widening of the market/industry definition. An SBU can choose to specialize, narrowing its market definition, and thus reducing the number of potential substitutes.

- **Bargaining power of suppliers.**
  The strength of suppliers in an industry will affect the attractiveness of that industry. An SBU can define its industry in order to minimize the influence of suppliers. For example, it can broaden its industry definition in order to include a greater number of suppliers and more substitute inputs in order to decrease its dependence on a single powerful supplier.

- **Bargaining power of buyers.**
  Market attractiveness is influenced by the power of buyers. The SBU can define its market in order to diffuse buyer influence; for example, widening the definition may enable the SBU to avoid powerful concentrated buyers.

- **Intensity of competition.**
  Rivalry in a market/industry is the result of competitors constantly seeking to improve their position. The manner in which the SBU defines its environment will determine the intensity of competition it will face. A narrow definition may place the SBU in a protected niche void of competition. In other instances, a narrow definition may place the SBU in direct confrontation with an extremely powerful competitor.

After having analyzed the relevant structural forces, the SBU will define its market/industry in a manner that will allow it to assume a defendable competitive position. These structural forces often exert influences in contradictory directions: one structural force may dictate broadening the market/industry definition in order to improve competitive position while the other will dictate narrowing. Thus the SBU will seek the best possible position in order to defend itself against competitive forces and to enable it to exercise influence over the balance of these forces. Another consideration in defining the scope of an SBU's market is its geographic dimension. Does the SBU compete in a market which is local, regional, national, or international? This question is of paramount importance, more so today than ever before; the strategic business area for many activities is continuously expanding as national borders become less and less significant.[23] The SBU must decide which geographic delineation will enable it to best assume a defendable competitive position.

The SBU and the market/industry have been presented here as they are the two most important concepts in this book. A typical chapter in this book will discuss the following concepts: planning focus; matrices – dimensions, grid, and cells; relevant strategic variables; use of model; model assumptions; and focus of analysis. Each is discussed below.

Planning focus

As a planning tool, each portfolio approach has a planning focus. A planning focus is the most important strategic aspect being analyzed and planned by the total portfolio matrix. Each portfolio approach differently places and depicts business units on its matrix. There are many lessons, and implications, relating to the exact location of a certain business unit on a portfolio matrix (which are elaborated upon below for each portfolio approach). However, the planning focus of a portfolio matrix is a pattern which emerges from the completed matrix on which all the corporation's business units appear. Examples of planning foci are:

- **Cash flow.**
  Models that have cash flow as their planning focus seek a balance between SBUs with a surplus in cash and SBUs that require cash.

- **Return on investment (ROI).**
  Approaches with ROI as their goal function depict investment strategies that endeavor to maximize the return on investment.

- **Risk/return ratio.**
  Models that concentrate upon the relationship between risk and return on investment present strategies for management in accordance with the desired degree of risk (risk averse, risk seekers).

- **Life cycle stage distribution.**
  Approaches that focus upon the life-cycle stage of the SBU's market serve as a planning apparatus that enables management to achieve the desired distribution of SBUs across life-cycle stages.

Multiobjective decision making

Some approaches maintain a single planning focus while others are based upon a combination of goal functions. Multicriteria or multiobjective planning requires that the corporate manager evaluate different foci simultaneously. Often the achievement of one goal comes at the expense of another. Unfortunately, there exists no trade-off function that can guide the manager to an optimal solution. Instead a satisfying or heuristic solution is sought.

Use and display of matrices

Dimensions

The typical portfolio matrix is two-dimensional, though some three-dimensional matrices have been developed and are used. The two axes are basic strategic characteristics (aspects) on which the different business units are scaled. Usually one dimension is external to the business unit (market or industry oriented), and the second is internal (competence or competitive position). The intersection of the paired values on the two axes determines the location of the specific business unit within the portfolio matrix; the coordinates in the two-dimensional representation. These two dimensions vary depending on the specific portfolio approach. For generalization and ease of use, we will term them the external/vertical axis (the Y axis) and the internal/horizontal axis (the X axis).

Grid

A portfolio grid is created when each continuous axis of the portfolio is divided into two or more parts. For example, a mid-point division of the two axes will result in a 2×2 grid (such as the BCG grid). Other examples are the 3×3 grid, and the non-symmetrical 3×5 grid.

By imposing the grid upon the two-dimensional representation of the portfolio we get the portfolio matrix (for the above examples we'll get 2×2, 3×3, and 3×5 matrices, respectively,). The matrix subdivides the total portfolio area into distinct areas – cells. For example, in a 2×2 matrix we have four different cells.

Cells

Business units located within one of the cells created by the grid have similar strategic characteristics, and are different from business units located in other areas of the matrix. Each classification on the matrix implies a different pattern for sales, assets, earnings, and cash flow over time. Depending on the specific portfolio matrix used, these strategic similarities may be recognized in the model by assigning a common generic name to the strategy (such as Cash Cows or Dogs), by recommending the same strategic action for the business units in the same cell (such as Divest, Double or quit), or both.

Relevant strategic variables

A strategic variable is defined in the context of the focal organization, partaking in its strategy. There are lists of tens and hundreds of strategic variables, but there is as yet no agreed-upon master list of these variables. More than two decades of research on organizational strategy has produced four groups of strategic variables, or metavariables, on which theory in the area rests. These metavariables are: Strategy, [24, 25, 26, 27, 28] Strategy Making, [29, 30, 31, 32, 33, 34] Structure, [35, 36, 37, 38, 39, 40, 41] and Environment[42, 43, 44, 45]. The fifth, and usually the dependent metavariable in strategic studies, is Performance. We have added a sixth metavariable, Basic Characteristics of the firm.

- **Environment.**
  The environment includes all factors outside the organization which affect or are affected by the strategic business unit. The environment includes both the unit's industry, which is its immediate environment, and the general, wider environment (international and national policies, the economy, other industries).

- **Strategy content.**
  The content of the strategy is the output of the strategy-making process. Most people refer to it as the strategy. It is the multifunctional posture of the organization in functional areas such as engineering, production, and marketing.

- **Strategy-making process.**
  Strategy-making process is an ongoing process whereby, intentionally or not, the organization's objectives and means to achieve them are determined; that is, the strategy formulation and implementation – both formal aspects (such as analysis) and informal aspects (such as risk and initiative).

- **Structure.**
  Structure is the deployment of management resources within the business unit. It is an important tool in strategy implementation, and a critical factor affecting strategy formulation; in other words, it is an integral part of strategy.

- **Performance.**
  Performance is the ultimate strategic dependent variable: the result of the major decisions taken to match the organization with its environment.

- **Basic characteristics.**
  Basic characteristics are the inherent outcomes of the organization's establishment, history, and past strategy. They affect and constrain strategy change and are difficult, if not impossible, to modify in the short run.

As a planning tool, each portfolio approach relates to some strategic variables. Its planning focus is usually a Performance strategic variable (cash flow, return on investment). Each of the two dimensions may be either one strategic variable, or a composite of many strategic variables. Usually the vertical/external dimension is related to the Environment (such as industry growth rate) and the horizontal/internal to the Strategy Content (R&D, distribution network coverage), Basic Characteristics (assets, sales), or to Performance (market share) of the business unit.

In each chapter relevant strategic variables for the portfolio model under discussion are listed. These variables are discussed when first encountered.

Objective vs. Subjective Data

The task of gathering data for the purpose of portfolio analysis presents a problem of availability and reliability.

Objective financial statistics for corporate business units are accessible from fairly reliable internal corporate sources. Financial data for the market/industry and competitors can be obtained through business intelligence sources and are generally somewhat less dependable. The reliability of all financial information becomes increasingly problematic as we move from historical through current to forecasted analyses. Thus even 'objective' data require some degree of subjective evaluation.

The vast majority of strategic variables require that the corporate manager quantify qualitative phenomena. As most measures are relative, the process requires conjecture, deduction, estimation, experimentation, guesstimation, interpretation, reasoning and speculation. Internal corporate and external industry experts may be consulted in order to alleviate the guesswork.

Use of the models

The portfolio matrix approach has several uses for the corporate manager – descriptive, analytical and prescriptive. Firstly, all models provide a means of visualizing the current competitive positioning of the strategic business units within the corporate portfolio according to external and internal dimensions.[46] Secondly, the matrix construct allows the corporate manager to identify the major strategic issues facing the corporation and to isolate some of the basic characteristics of the strategy of each SBU.

On the basis of the above analysis, the various models provide tools for the formulation of corporate and business strategies to be implemented in order to improve overall portfolio performance. The matrix approach also enables the corporate manager to evaluate the success of corporate and business strategies by allowing him/her to compare actual future positioning with planned or projected positioning.

Finally, the approach can serve as a key tool in competitor analysis as it allows the corporate manager to visualize and identify competitor corporate strategy.

It should be noted that not all models are equally skillful in all the uses outlined above. As some models are better than others, the corporate manager should choose approaches carefully; in some cases he/she may wish to use two or more models in stages in order to benefit from the strength of each in different uses. This topic is discussed in Chapter 10.

Assumptions

A portfolio approach is based on a world view – Weltanschauung, as the Germans call it. The developers of the model have to approach the very complex world of corporate strategy from a focused and manageable point of view, otherwise the task is unfeasible. Each portfolio matrix is built upon a theory, research, a body of knowledge and a relevant discipline. For us, and for managers using this portfolio, these are the assumptions on which the matrix is built. If we accept the assumptions and if the conditions for which the model was developed hold true in our situation, we will use the model. Even when the assumptions do not exactly hold true in a certain situation, the model can still be used, discounting for the deviations from its basic view of the world.

Focus of analysis

The corporation may be considered a hierarchy of portfolios. Each level – corporate, group, division and SBU – can be regarded as a portfolio with constituents of the next level as its unit of analysis. At each level of the corporation, portfolio theory can be implemented for analysis and planning purposes. The corporate portfolio is comprised of divisions. The division portfolio in turn is an aggregation of SBUs. Haspeslagh[47] points out that in practice an SBU is rarely a single homogeneous unit; thus it too can be considered a portfolio. On the disaggregate level, smaller units within the SBU, such as individual products or product lines, are examined. We refer to two levels only: Corporate and SBU. However, the portfolio matrix approach may be applied to any level or focus of analysis.

2

The first corporate portfolio model: BCG

History: Development and use

The growth-share matrix, generally known as the BCG (Boston Consulting Group) matrix, was the first corporate portfolio matrix developed. This two-dimensional presentation of business unit positions, determined by market growth rate and relative market share, had an immediate and profound effect on corporate strategy making in the USA and the world.

The development of the BCG matrix was an outgrowth of the work done by the Boston Consulting Group (founded by Bruce D. Henderson) on experience-curve effects, which indicated that variable cost per unit decreases by 10% to 30% every time production experience (accumulated volume) is doubled. Some of this work was done as early as 1965.[1] BCG found that in any market segment of an industry, price levels tend to be very similar for similar products; therefore, what makes one company more profitable than the next must be the levels of its costs.[2] The other corner-stone for the BCG growth-share matrix is the product life cycle concept

19

which has been with us for many decades.[3] Its graphs show the rise, stabilization and decline over time of product sales for all competitors combined, as well as the number of competitors and industry profits.

The early empirical basis of the experience-curve for the BCG model was a longitudinal study of 24 products in seven industries: electric power, consumer durables, plastics, consumer nondurables, petroleum, nonferrous metals, and electric parts. This study focused on the cost-to-price relationship which results from the experience-curve.[4] Thus, BCG's work is empirically based but its importance is more conceptual than empirical.[5]

The BCG experience-curve and growth-share matrix took America by storm. Experience-curves became the key concept in corporate headquarters. By 1970 the BCG approach had been used in more than 100 companies.[6] In the late 1970s, a respected merger specialist reported that the BCG concept of market leadership was becoming increasingly important for companies on the prowl for acquisitions. In Spring 1977, Mitchell-Hutchins, a respected firm on The Street (and later part of Paine, Weber), issued a lengthy report suggesting that its clients analyze corporations along much the same lines as those espoused by BCG.[7] A few years after its introduction most of the Fortune 1000 corporations were complete BCG converts, or were looking at their businesses in this way.[8] During the decade 1973–83, BCG averaged a 25% annual increase in billings.[9]

The BCG model is the least complex of all its subsequent mutations. It is simple and inexpensive in measurement and application, and easily understandable as a tool to present findings and discuss their strategic implications at board meetings.[10, 11] It also rests (as far as this is possible) on solid theoretical and empirical foundations. Thus, it has become the best known and most widely used portfolio model, and at the same time the most frequently criticized one.

The planning focus: Cash flow

The planning focus of the BCG portfolio matrix is the cash flow provided to or extracted from each of the business units comprising the corporation.[12] Cash generation and use is a strong function of market growth rate and relative market share. The growth rate of a business unit affects the rate at which it will use cash. The experience-curve position relative to competitors will affect the margins and the rate at which a business unit generates cash. The sources of, and need for, cash should be balanced without jeopardizing market position.[13] The thrust of the BCG matrix, in its ultimate prescriptions, is to balance the cash flows among the various business units and thereby develop and meet the growth objectives of the corporation, while simultaneously accommodating its cash requirements.

During the middle and late stages of their life cycle, successful business units generate cash, which in turn should be invested in business units which are anticipated to be the major future cash generators. This is a continuous process since, if implemented successfully, in years to come these newly successful business units will generate cash to be invested in yet newer promising businesses.[14, 15]

At the business level the BCG assumption is that the primary objectives of an organization are growth and profitability, leading to four strategic choices regarding the market share growth of an SBU:

1.   To increase market share,

2.   To hold market share,

3.   To harvest,

4.   To divest.[16]

Use and display

Dimensions

In the BCG model, the external/vertical axis is the market growth rate, representing the industry attractiveness (product/market attractiveness). Growth is important for three reasons:

1.   When a market (an industry) is growing at a high rate rather than a low rate, it is easier to improve one's market share.[17] Market share can be improved by obtaining the largest share of the growth, without forcing other competitors to operate at a lower fraction of their current capacity.

2.   A common perception is that growth businesses promise future returns on investment.

3.   A high market growth rate generally has adverse effects on the cash flow of the business, even when profitability is high. Thus, the overall growth rate of the market served became a strategic variable in the BCG grid. In the BCG model, the annual overall served-market growth rate percentage is plotted on the vertical axis. This dimension is typically calibrated on a linear percentage scale of –10% to 30%. The rate may be an average of recent past, current, and/or expected future data.

The internal/horizontal axis represents the business unit's relative competitive strength, measured by its relative market share, as a ratio of the business unit's sales volume to the sales volume of its largest competitor in the market served. The scale is logarithmic. It should be noted that the customary presentation of the BCG is of *decreasing* market share from left to right: those units with a high relative market share are located near the vertical axis, while units with a low relative market share are located away from the vertical axis. The vertical axis is presented in the conventional way, with the higher values at the top.

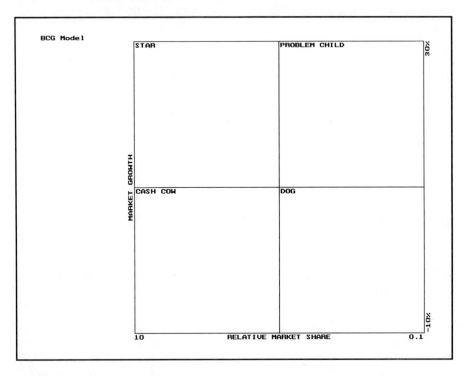

Figure 2.1   BCG model.

Grid

The BCG model is a two-by-two grid, in which business units are plotted as circles on the two-dimensional layout of market growth rate vs. relative market share. Each circle in the display represents a business. In our examples, the size of the circle is proportional to the total size of the market (SBU and its competitors), and the relative size of the business unit is represented by the shaded area of the circle (the pie), which is usually made proportional to sales, though sometimes to assets. The most generally used measure for industry growth is volume growth. The external/vertical market growth rate axis is divided into high growth and low growth, the dividing line commonly being set, rather arbitrarily, at ten percent. Anything below this level is termed low market growth rate, above it – high.

As noted above, the internal/vertical scale is logarithmic. Competitive position (that is, sales relative to the major competitor) is plotted on a logarithmic scale since it is related to the experience-curve effects which are fundamental to the BCG concept (when cost per unit is plotted on a log–log scale against cumulative total units, the resulting plot is a straight line). A typical range for the ratio is 0.1 to 10. The line dividing high and low competitive position should be set at 1.0, on the grounds that a ratio over 1.0 means that our firm is the market leader, and has a competitive advantage on the experience-curve and in economies of scale over any and all competitors. A ratio under 1.0 means that somebody else has the advantage. In practice some authors require a ratio over 1.5 for 'high' competitive strength in high-growth markets, where there is still some jockeying for position. This is due to the observation that in such markets nearly-equal competitive positions may lead to cutthroat competition, impeding the cash-generation potential of the business.

Thus, the resulting grid has four distinct areas/cells/boxes:

- High market growth rate/high relative market share,

- Low market growth rate/high relative market share,

- High market growth rate/low relative market share,

- Low market growth rate/low relative market share.

The BCG model goes one step further, introducing the 'BCG Zoo'. It assigns a generic name to all business units located within each of the four areas of the grid. Of course, a business unit can fall near or upon a border between these categories. So, in the order presented above we have:

- Stars,

- Cash Cows,

- Question Marks (sometimes referred to as 'Problem Children'),

- Dogs.

The four types are described briefly as follows:

Stars are business units that have a relatively large market share and operate in fast-growing markets. These are usually new units in growing industries, with resulting high profits. They are leaders in their industry and generate relatively large revenues from sales, though they are frequently in rough balance with respect to bottom-line net cash flow, since they require large investments in fixed and working capital to ensure high growth rate in a growing market.

Cash Cows have, in the past, gained large market shares, but they currently compete in industries whose growth rate has slowed down. They usually are the Stars of the past, which today supply the corporation with enough profits to maintain the current market position. Cash generation is good and cash needs are minimal. These businesses can generate large cash surpluses. They form the foundation of the corporation, providing the cash flow necessary to pursue other strategic goals.

Question Marks compete in a growth market but they have a relatively small market share. This combination leads to increasing amounts of investments to defend their (small) share of the market and secure survival. High growth requires cash to support it, but the Question Marks have difficulty generating cash because of their low share. They are net users of cash, and will probably remain that way unless measures are taken to improve their market share. There are significant uncertainties about these units: they might be very profitable or not. Without substantial investment they are very likely to become Dogs.

Dogs are small-market-share business units in non-growing industries, condemned to low profits. Net cash flow is typically small and frequently negative. Any move to gain market share is forcefully counterattacked by the dominant competitors. These Dogs are low-profit business units – frequently losers which require large investments of top management time and skill to keep them alive.

Relevant strategic variables

To use the BCG model, values for the following variables should be assigned:

- Market growth rate (for Y axis),
- Relative market share (for X axis).

Market growth rate

Definition: This is a current-year measurement based on data for two or three consecutive years: current total sales vs. last year's or the year before last's total sales.

Relative market share

Definition: This is a log-linear transformation of the ratio between the SBU's sales and the sales of the leading competitor (the industry leader, or if the SBU under analysis is the leader, then the the second largest competitor).

Use of the model

The main use of the BCG matrix is for cash balancing. Since every corporation is active in the financial market there is no requirement that the portfolio be perfectly balanced at all times. Short-term excess funds are appropriately invested when they are available. Also, there are accepted financial strategies for a corporation facing a permanent change in the level of its funding requirements. Depending on the corporation's preferred financial risk level (and market opportunities), long-term loans and stock issues are used for raising additional funds.

Sometimes, as in cases of mature products or shrinking markets, a corporation may face permanent excess funds, with no use in the current strategic array. Theoretically, the corporation should return these funds to its stockholders for reinvestment in other ventures. But managerial behavior, and tax laws, usually trigger a search for new investments (entry into new industries, market segments, countries, and so on).

However, even with all these financial tools and strategies, over time significant cash-flow imbalances within the corporation are not viable. Since the growth-share matrix is fundamentally aimed at the balancing of cash flows, the matrix may be of most use to companies that must operate with limited cash resources.

An abundance of Stars in the portfolio may sound very attractive, but it will require a constant stream of investment for several years to come. Considering the lag between the initial development of a product/market business (from innovation, to application, to building a market), investment may continue for five to ten years before the business unit starts generating substantial positive cash flows (if ever!). Most corporations cannot support an unbalanced Star-heavy portfolio.

Moreover, even if financial requirements can be met, other resources such as skilled labor, equipment, plant, and particularly additional management skills and time, are constantly being invested in the Stars. The end result is that these corporations deplete their resources and are taken over by unbalanced 'Cash-Cow-heavy portfolio' corporations with the resources (financial and managerial) to maintain Stars. Every high-paced product/ market innovation firm faces these problems, and they are especially prevalent in high-technology industries. In these businesses, life cycles become increasingly short, products are aimed at specific markets which are getting narrower and narrower, while the investments in innovation, application, production, market development, and sales are staggering.

When the portfolio is Cash Cow tilted, the corporation's very future is at stake. Though cash is generously available, such a portfolio indicates a near-term demise, since Cash Cows tend to eventually dry out. Cash-Cow-heavy corporations with scant future alternatives in their portfolio are doomed to stagnation and consolidation.

Thus, corporations heavy with Cash Cows are usually engaged in a frantic search for Stars (by acquisition, or in-house development); they are ready to pay large multiples of current earnings to acquire Stars, in an effort to attain future stability and growth. In addition to defining the present growth-share positions of each of the business units within the company, and thereby helping to guide the generation of alternative sets of investment actions, matrices should be created that express the expected future growth-share situations under given action scenarios.

A first goal is to protect the position of the Cash Cows, but to guard against excessive investment in these business units. The first priority for usage of cash from the Cash Cows is to support the Stars that are not self-sustaining. However, remember that: 'If at any point a business (Cash Cow or Star) has a higher value to someone outside the corporation than to the parent company the SBU should be sold.'[18] The second priority is to work on the development of future Stars (for example, product R&D). The third priority for this cash is to fund a number of promising Question Marks in order to move them to dominant positions as Stars in their industries. The Question Marks that cannot or should not be funded are candidates for divestment. It may be hard to find interested buyers for a Question Mark, and if so the price will be low. It may be better to simply hold on to it, especially if it requires little of the corporation's management resources.[18]

Dogs can sometimes be made viable by specializing the business unit into a niche which it can dominate. Otherwise, a significant increase in share may be an expensive proposition. Other alternatives are managing the business unit for cash, cutting off all investment, or divesting it. The overall strategy is to strike a balance such that the cash generated by the Cash Cows, plus that from the divestment of Question Marks and Dogs, is sufficient to support the Stars and to fund selected Question Marks in moves to dominant positions in their industries.[19]

The BCG approach recommends setting market-share objectives early in the product life cycle, gaining and maintaining market share through growth phases, and only in maturity sacrificing market share objectives for cash.[20, 21]

The (implied) optimal strategy for a business unit is to be in a strong market-share position when the market matures. Balancing a portfolio means continuous efforts to keep Stars on course and turn some of the Question Marks into Stars, which the ever-progressing life cycle will eventually turn into Cash Cows. This is accompanied by housecleaning of Dogs when they have really proved to be expendable.

This may be done by using the BCG model. Each business unit is classified on the two-dimensional matrix: product/market attractiveness (growth rate) and the business unit competitive strength. The unit size is also noted. Different business units, sometimes very diversified in nature, are uniformly presented, using a single measurement system. By plotting a current portfolio on the BCG matrix a pattern emerges. The pattern reveals current cash-generation and cash-use tendencies. Expected future positions, and thus some notion of overall value to the corporation, can be plotted and assessed on the grid as well.[22]

It is important to note that the BCG model is not confined to large corporations. The concept applies to small firms as well. In large firms the portfolio can consist of businesses and products in several industries and markets. In a small firm the portfolio revolves around products and markets.[23] Thus the BCG model can be used for various sizes and structures of organizations.

There are strategic choices inherent in each cell of the BCG grid.[24, 25]

- **Stars:**
  Hold (or sometimes even increase) market share.

- **Question Marks:**
  Increase market share, or harvest/divest.

- **Cash Cows:**
  Hold or add market share.

- **Dogs:**
  Harvest/divest/liquidate.

Harvey[26] stresses that managers must suit the chosen strategy for each SBU, where a Star mission is associated with an 'analytical' type of manager, a Cash Cow with an 'engineer' type, a Problem Child with a 'salesman' type, and a Dog with a 'cost accountant' type. The important point is the fit between the style and the strategic mission.

Another use of the BCG model, briefly mentioned above, is for displaying the corporate portfolio at separate points in time, to see changes in possible directions.[27] It can be useful for assessing the congruence of actual strategies with planned strategies.

The BCG model can also be used to plot the portfolio of a competitor, and thereby learn the competitor's strategy. Porter[28] has noted that when using the growth-share matrix for competitor analysis, if the competitor is known to use the growth-share portfolio approach in planning, the predictive power of the analysis is all the greater.

Model assumptions, criticisms, limits of use

The BCG model assumes that higher market share leads to higher profits.[29] The PIMS project, and mainly the studies by Buzzell *et al.*,[30] show that market share is highly correlated with profitability, but to a lesser degree than projected by the early work with the BCG model. Henderson[31] claimed that intuition and experience had made him aware of the relationships between market share and return on investment, and that for him PIMS merely confirmed what he knew all along. The BCG matrix is based on striving for a dominant market share while the industry is in its early growth stage.

The very basic assumptions of the BCG model are:

- High growth rate → implies opportunities,

- High market share → implies strength.[32]

BCG assumes that the primary objectives of an organization are growth and profitability.[33] BCG also assumes that SBUs are independent. If they are interdependent (for example, a Dog and a Cash Cow share production facilities), the model is invalid.[34]

After moving along the industry life cycle, net cash flows reach their peak when the market reaches maturity, and the business unit with the dominant market share at that time has the highest margins, and, of course, profits. The assumption is that at the mature stage of the product life cycle the firm with the highest market share has the most experience, the lowest costs, and is, hence, the most profitable and, assuming no major reinvestment, a high cash generator.[35] This rationale is based on the second assumption of the BCG model: the experience-curve.

Experience-curve theory lies behind the growth-share matrix. This theory assumes that costs decrease by a certain characteristic percentage each time that a doubling occurs in the cumulative number of units manufactured, distributed and sold. Experience-curve principles have taught that when the number of times a task is performed doubles, the variable cost of performing that task declines by approximately 20 percent.[36] The experience-curve concept observes that overall costs associated with a product line decline with time in the manner of learning-curve behavior. In the early studies of experience-curve effects, costs (or sometimes only the value-added portion) in certain industries appeared to go down about 10% to 30%[37] whenever total cumulative product experience doubled (in quantity, not time!). When cost per unit is plotted on a log–log scale against cumulative total units, the resulting plot is a straight line. Later studies reduced this cost advantage estimate for many industries. Unlike the old learning-curve (which applied only to employee productivity), the experience-curve has no thresholds, and is applied to ALL functions: purchasing, production, accounting, marketing, and the like. The combination of the economies of scale (total annual volume) and the experience-curve effect (total cumulative volume) can have a dramatic impact on the cost position of a firm by diminishing overall costs by some given percentage. This ability to reduce costs over time accords a quantifiable value to market share, which thus became a strategic variable in the BCG grid, on account of the inference that long-range profitability and cash generation are functions of market share because of the reduced costs. In a mature market, the dominant firm – the largest-volume competitor – will have the lowest costs, and hence, the highest profits. As already noted, market share and profitability have been shown to be strongly related. On the average, businesses whose absolute market shares exceed 50% are more than three times as profitable as businesses with absolute shares of less than 10%. However, the economies of scale, although substantial, are typically smaller than those which were associated with the experience-curve discussions of the early 1970s.[38]

The experience-curve concept resulted in an empirical hypothesis ('The Rule of Three and Four'): 'A stable competitive market never has more than three significant competitors, the largest of which has no more than four times the market share of the smallest.'[39, 40] The experience-curve concept emphasizes cost discontinuities between different products and different markets, including geographic markets.[41]

Another assumption is that industries, markets, business units, products (or services), and market shares can be neatly defined. Thus, the BCG concept is very sensitive, as are all portfolio matrices, to the definition of a business unit as a unique product/market segment. Also, the quantification of a position in the market is highly sensitive to the product/market definition. By defining the served market in different ways, the SBU can change its position from one quadrant to another, from market leader to minor competitor. There is an underlying assumption that the corporation is a closed system that must internally fund its cash flows.[42] This problematic issue is discussed above in the Use of the Model section.

Limitations

The main limitation of the growth-share matrix is that by itself it is not very useful in determining strategy for a particular business. The advice to 'harvest' or 'grow into a Star' is far from sufficient to guide managerial action.[43] In order to decide on operational strategies other models must be utilized in addition to the BCG model.

There are a number of barriers to implementation that could lead to misuse of the model. It might be hard or even impossible to sell off a Dog (no buyers), meaning that other solutions, not found in the BCG model, must be pursued.

The BCG model uses raw-experience theory, but ignores shared experience. The idea of shared experience suggests that careful attention must be paid to the possibility of continuing to gain experience in a low profit area in order to lower costs in a related, but more profitable, business – probably a Star or a Cash Cow.[44] Another common barrier to implementation occurs when a business is identified as a Cash Cow or Dog, or placed in a harvest/divest category. A fairly common value system amongst managers is that growth and progress are normal for all businesses. Thus, a business identified as one to be run down for cash generation is alien to management values. Moreover, the harvest position is soon recognized by the work force, who tend to become demotivated and resistant to management policies. Strong pressure may be mounted by both management and the employee force to reinvest in the cash generating business, which may be exactly the reverse of central management's intended strategy.[45]

Misuse of the BCG model

The main misuse of the model is viewing it as a prescriptive strategy maker. Use of the BCG model does not substitute for business-level strategy making, and it does not dictate a strategy. It is merely a description (or representation) of current situations or future prospects as evaluated on the basis of certain available data. Strategy is yet to be decided upon. Sharplin notes that the BCG model could lead to misdetermination of strategies. He states that strategy should be chosen by market forces and not solely by the position on the BCG grid.[46]

The growth-share matrix is best applied to portfolios whose business units make items in large quantities, and which compete strongly in simple, unsophisticated markets based on strict price competition.[47] In such markets competitive strategies are based on early embarkment on the learning-curve. Therefore, only in such industries do relative costs strongly determine success.[48] In some product–market situations, the customer's needs are more complex, and can be met by a number of alternative products/technologies.[49] In these markets relative costs are less important than other marketing variables. Day[50] limited even further the use of the BCG matrix, claiming that the experience-curve only holds in high-volume industries. According to Aaker,[51] the experience-curve model has been most successfully applied in situations of high growth, high value-added, continuous-process manufacturing, and capital-intensive industries. It is less useful in mature industries where the curve is almost flat; in industries where purchased raw materials represent most of the costs; in mining and forestry; and most of all in service industries. It is also of limited use in highly volatile high-tech businesses, where new technologies may emerge before experience-based costs become a decisive competitive factor.

Real growth could be obscured by several factors that must be taken into consideration while evaluating the growth of an industry. These factors (such as inflation, cyclicity) must be neutralized by calculations via base numbers.

One general effect of inflation is that it tends to make even low-real-growth businesses into apparent high-growth operations. In addition, depreciation allowances are quite inadequate to cope with the costs of replacing capital assets. As a result, especially for capital-intensive businesses, 'high inflation can seriously transform the actual cash-flow characteristics of a theoretically balanced portfolio, resulting in potentially dangerous liquidity positions.'[52]

Many businesses are cyclical and the cycle must be clearly understood, using a long enough time span to assess real growth rate. Otherwise, all the systems can give potentially misleading positioning. 'Strategic portfolio systems must not be used as short-term or even medium-term forecasting models.'[52] Industries with a short life cycle are dangerous arenas for using the BCG model. The Cash Cow position is based on a long maturity phase of the life cycle. If, however, this phase turns out to be short-lived, then the whole policy of investing in Question Mark and Star products in the anticipation of a financial return from Cash Cows is misplaced.[53]

Criticism

Being the first, the BCG portfolio matrix drew the heaviest fire from critics. In fact, the use of 'portfolio planning' in general as the predominant contributor to strategy formulation has been criticized, especially the indiscriminate use of the growth-share matrix.[54] Criticism generally falls into one or more of the following categories:

1. The definition of the market (and consequently the market share) for the products of the business unit is fuzzy. A slight change in definition can cause a significant change in assessed market share, and therefore in the appearance of the matrix.

2. Relative to other variables, the importance of market share as a causal contributor to cash flow, profits, and competitive advantage is overemphasized.[55] With the BCG matrix, many variables affecting profitability (other than market growth rate and relative market share) are generally ignored.[56, 57]

3. The experience-curve effect applies to a lesser and lesser degree as we move from consideration of competitive, high-volume markets to consideration of other types of markets.

4. A high growth rate is only one measure of the attractiveness of a market.[58, 59, 60]

5. The simple, prescriptive properties of the matrix stimulate portfolio actions that may or may not in fact be productive. This is mainly because it is too narrow and provides a myopic view of the strategic position and options.[61]

From a purely economic point of view, the BCG model assumes that the lowest cost competitor has the highest rate of return. This should be true. However, the focus on cost economics holds true only if all costs are taken into account, including opportunity costs of management.[62] In practice, it is impossible to pinpoint, take into account, and quantify all cost elements. Also, the prescriptive approach does not take into account risks stemming from the environment, particularly the actions of competitors.

The cash-flow assumptions of the BCG matrix are not always supported in practice. In the PIMS data, 59% of the Dogs and 54% of the Question Marks were net cash generators; 26% of the Cash Cows and 28% of the Stars were net cash users.[63]

A frequently heard criticism of the growth-share matrix is the degree to which it assumes that a company is locked into internally generated cash flow.[64] Other models discuss the debt policy of corporations as a whole.[65]

The BCG approach assumes that it is easier to increase market share in a high-growth business than in a low-growth business. Wensley[66] claimed that the assumption that in a high-growth market competition will be less aggressive than in a mature market is naive. He postulates that a rational competitor will react strongly to volume gains above market share. Even though in such a benevolent market competitors may only be gaining in nominal volume while losing share, they are still acutely conscious of the opportunities lost to the competitor. The main question remains, of course, whether the competitors also view the market as a fast-growing one, and incorporate this view of it into their plans. If the competitors have differing expectations, a less aggressive response is to be expected.

The BCG model emphasizes cost effectiveness, and the fact that it is achieved at the expense of flexibility.[67]

How do you take into account shared experience between various business units? (The success of a business unit may be strongly related to synergism with other business units within the corporation.)

There are exceptions to the general rule that small market share is associated with low profitability, since variables other than market share have a strong influence. The BCG matrix ignores the fact that there are SBUs with low market share that enjoy profits and growth rates higher than their dominant market rivals.[68]

Abell and Hammond[69] claimed that where experience or scale effects are small, low-share competitors have different cost curves than high-share competitors, because of differences in technology. Woo and Cooper[70] examined the strategies of successful businesses that hold a low market share. Some of the characteristics that they observed were relatively high quality, narrow product basis, and low overall costs. Thus, there are successful competitive strategies that do not involve market dominance. In addition to his generic low cost leadership strategy, Porter[71] suggested at least two other successful strategies, differentiation and focus. Both these strategies are LOW market share strategies. The focus strategy, later divided into two different strategies, focus–costs and focus–differentiation, is an especially low market share strategy, though with profits above the industry average. Aaker[72] points out that the experience-curve is not relevant for focus strategies. There are two additional strategies that are suitable for firms operating in declining markets: leadership and niche. The conditions appropriate to them are not revealed by the simple growth-share matrix alone. These strategies allow the SBU to retain a Cash Cow position in what would otherwise be a Dog situation.

Thus, the BCG's narrow view of the Question Mark/Star/Cash Cow cycle may be misleading in many situations and trigger unprofitable strategic actions. Dogs may be friends, Cows provide more than milk, and Stars may have already burned themselves out. PIMS has found that the best relative market-share variable to use is market share relative to the sum of the three largest competitors.[73] Is market share a good surrogate for competitive position? It is a better surrogate in stable markets than in unstable markets.

According to BCG, Dogs are meant for harvest/divest/liquidation, though the low-profit businesses may be used to gain valuable experience that can help to lower costs on Stars and Cows.[74] In addition, some of the BCG prescriptions could ultimately lead to a lack of innovative product introductions, since, by definition, new products start out as Dogs or as Question Marks. BCG does not acknowledge that new products could be Dogs. Thus, it inadequately represents new businesses in new markets that are just starting to grow; Hofer and Schendel realized this and added the development stage to the life cycle.[75]

The use of highs and lows is too simplistic. Middle positions are needed.[76] This oversimplicity was the basis for developing new models such as the GE model and the DPM model.

Richard Rumelt of UCLA has noted that, although the underlying factors of the 'experience-curve' theory are well established, their application is not so straightforward.[77] The electronics industry appears to be an environment where reality fits this model, but it is not so clear in other markets, characterized by high segmentation, or with heavy branding and promotion. The competitor with the most experience may be the 'oldest' competitor in the industry. If this older firm has a dedicated plant and/or dedicated equipment, it may not be able to exploit new cost-reducing technology as easily as an emerging competitor. Lowering costs may be effected by shared experience obtained in other related product–market segments as well as by accumulated output. In other words, the experience of a corporation cannot be measured independently for each product–market segment. Other factors important to lowering (or raising) costs could be external factors, technology breakthroughs, and other events.[78]

Rowe, Mason and Dickel[79] have noted two gross misuses/oversights of the BCG model. In some cases it may be perfectly logical for a small competitor in a mature market to strive for a larger market share (for example, for another 2% to 3%). If one strictly adheres to the BCG concept, the prescription would be non-growth objectives, since the SBU at hand is competitively weak and in a low-growth market.

On the other hand, the BCG model implies that SBUs should strive to be monopolies – any business should obtain the highest market share possible. This attitude completely ignores the fact that governments object to monopolies and have set laws to prohibit their existence. The model's basic content is straightforward. The advantages lie in having a good product ready to market earlier than one's rivals and in having the financial and organizational strength to sustain more rapid growth (at perhaps a lower margin!) than one's rivals. Like all frame models, the BCG model does not address the issue of gaining these advantages in the first place.[80]

Variations and additions

When the growth-share matrix is divided into cells, the position of the division between the Cash Cows and the Dogs is sometimes arbitrary for relative market shares between 1.0 and 1.5.[81] The definition of the market-share variable changes somewhat from one situation to another. In many cases the horizontal axis is strictly 'relative market share' in accordance with the original experience-curve concepts. However, for those situations in which it is believed that competitive cost advantage is gained from more than one experience factor, the horizontal axis can become 'weighted relative competitive position,' or just 'relative competitive position'. In some businesses with complicated economic factors the ratio should represent relative cost position as a weighted average of the business unit's relative position in each separate cost area.[82, 83]

Two alternative names that have been used for the Question Marks are 'Problem Children' and 'Wildcats'. The Mead Corporation proposed other names: Sweepstake (Question Marks), Savings Account (Stars), Bond (Cash Cows), Mortgage (Dogs). They also added the risk inherent to each cell: Sweepstake – extremely high risk, Savings Account – medium risk, Bond – low risk, Mortgage – medium risk.[84]

It is possible to incorporate means to display sequences (or paths) of circles on the display such that users can observe actual or projected changes over time in the size or location of a circle representing a strategic business unit.

It is possible to use the technique at more than one level of an organiza-tion. For example, for a large corporation, each circle may represent a division (a multiplicity of business units may blur the matrix if they are all plotted). Later, a circle representing a division of the corporation may be blown up to a growth-share matrix in which the constituent business units within each division are plotted, taking into account the market characte-ristics for each of the business units. This less aggregated view may provide useful insight into what is really going on within each division. In turn, the circle for each of the business units can be blown up to a growth-share matrix for product lines within a business unit.

Other 2×2 matrices have been developed that are similar to the growth-share matrix in that the plotting method uses two discrete variables (not composite variables). In this discussion these matrices are treated as elaborations of the BCG approach. (The major portfolio planning systems that appeared after the BCG growth-share matrix tend to use composite variables on each of the axes and are considered to be new approaches rather than elaborations of the BCG approach; the composite variables are generated from a number of variables.) Some examples of alternative discrete variables in various 2×2 matrices are:

Y Variable	X Variable
Market growth rate (%/yr)	Sales growth rate (%/yr)
Profitability growth rate (%/yr)	Profit on sales (%)
Profitability growth rate (%/yr)	Sales growth rate (%/yr)
Sales growth rate (%/yr)	Relative market share

These variations provide visual imagery but typically do not divide the matrix into boxes that suggest prescriptions based upon the position of a circle within the display.

In general, the additional 2×2 matrices with discrete variables permit the analysis of a portfolio in more dimensions than can be provided by the basic growth-share matrix. They are relatively simple to produce and can be used to display variables that are of unique concern to a given company. For example, the first of the above matrices displays how well the growth of the various business units matches the growth of their respective markets. No particular action is suggested in the general case, but in a specific case this measure may be of significant interest.

The sales portfolio is the one corporations usually use, such that the size of a circle depends upon the sales of the business unit. It is possible to develop portfolios whose circles represent profit streams, cash flows, or technology.[85]

Another 2×2 model uses RONA (return on net assets) and reinvestment. Henderson and Zakon,[86] both from the BCG, have extended the model to show the percent of reinvestment in each SBU. The percent of reinvestment is the growth rate divided by RONA (return on net assets). They display the reinvestment in a 2×2 matrix which has market growth rate on the Y axis and RONA on the X axis.

Reinvestment in a business depends on the market growth, the individual business growth, the aggressiveness employed to gain relative share, the returns from selling share and the relative competitive position.

One of the main additions is use of the BCG model for 'What if' scenarios. It is recommended that equivalent portfolio displays be developed for three to five years in the future to show the projected positions of the business units, given different investment decisions at the present, and different managerial performance in the future. These projected displays should be evaluated in terms of an overall corporate strategy. Hosmer[87] suggests a 'What if' type of evaluation, assuming different strategy decisions and assuming various levels of performance to evaluate the possible outcomes of different scenarios.

BCG's 'new' matrix in 1986 was the 'strategic environment matrix' in which the axes represent potential sources of advantage relative to competition (many vs. few), and the magnitude of the advantage (small vs. large).

This divides the competitive environment into four types: stalemate, fragmented, specialization, and volume.[88]

Another dimension of the BCG approach is to balance between the degree of risk and the profit fluctuation acceptable to the corporation. For example, companies in mature markets will probably try to shift investment into newer growth fields.[89]

3

The GE/McKinsey model

History: Development and use

The GE/McKinsey matrix, first developed in the early 1970s by General Electric and McKinsey & Co., had, by the early 1980s, become the most popular of the multifactor portfolio approaches to strategic planning. Haspeslagh[1] estimated that, as of 1979, 36% of the Fortune 1000 and 45% of the Fortune 500 industrial companies had introduced portfolio planning to some extent, and that 25 to 30 organizations had joined the user ranks each year in the period 1977–81.

The GE/McKinsey two-dimensional, nine-cell presentation of SBU positioning was developed out of a need to compare many and diverse businesses. An important aspect of this approach is that it not only considers objective factors (such as sales, profit and ROI), but also gives weight to subjectively estimated factors (such as volatility of market share, technology, employee loyalty, competitive stance, and social need).

The many names by which the matrix has been known are indicative of its history, purpose, and nature. The name most often used, the 'GE/McKinsey matrix', indicates its sources, General Electric and McKinsey & Co.[2] 'The Strategic Planning Grid', the original name given to the first version of the matrix by General Electric, suggests its basic purpose of strategic corporate planning of the SBUs. More descriptive titles are the 'Market Attractiveness–Competitive Position Matrix'; the 'Industry Attractiveness–Business Position Portfolio Model'; the 'Nine-Cell Business Screen Developed by General Electric'; and the 'Bubble Chart'. The first two names describe the labels given to the X and Y axes of the matrix. The third name reflects the breakdown of the matrix into nine cells with different strategic connotations. The last name, the 'Bubble Chart', is a graphic description of the pictorial representation of the SBUs as 'bubbles' or circles on the grid.

The original matrix, called the 'Strategic Planning Grid', was developed in the early 1970s by General Electric as part of an attempt to solve the problem of sorting and comparing its 43 separate and distinct major businesses. The grid was seen as a breakthrough because it provided a partial solution to the problem of finding a common comparative strategic base for businesses that were diverse and disparate in nature. As GE's Senior Vice-President for Corporate Strategic Planning put it: 'Some type of corporate glue was necessary.'[3] It was the recognition of this need that led to the planning work that drew these decentralized businesses together under a single strategic umbrella. Whereas the business units were charged with doing their own planning, strategic decisions concerning issues such as trade-offs and intra-SBU resource allocations were to be made at the corporate level. The interplay of the two separate functions enabled the functioning of the GE system as a whole.

Also, by quantifying subjective factors and including them in the analysis, the grid provided the decision maker with more decision-relevant information. Granted, it was still the corporate manager who ultimately decided on which strategies to take. But now, with the help of the strategic planning grid, he or she was better able to sort and compare disparate businesses. In the words of the GE Senior Vice-President: 'It's one way to compare apples and oranges.' Even though definitive weights were not given to the nonnumerical factors, the end result of using the matrix was a semi-quantitative positioning of the SBUs.

One of the main benefits of the GE model is that different weights can be given to the various factors (components of the X and Y axes) according to their specific importance in determining success for each SBU and its industry, making the assessment of each SBU more precise.[4] A company that used portfolio planning would typically employ a market attractiveness–competitive position matrix to classify SBUs.

The planning focus: Investment

The planning focus of the GE/McKinsey matrix is future profit, or the future return on investment. In other words, the main thrust of the planning of the matrix is the profit implications of short-term additional investment in each SBU.

As noted above, SBUs are rated as candidates for future investment in terms of both quantifiable and nonquantifiable elements. That is, for an SBU to be considered a 'winner' or good future investment, not only are sales, profit, and ROI considered (that is, the strictly quantitative elements) but various other factors, such as volatility of market share, technology, employee loyalty, competitive stance, and social need (that is, elements that are less readily quantifiable) as well.

Use and display of the matrix

Dimensions

The X and Y axes of the GE/McKinsey matrix represent overall measures of market (or industry) attractiveness and relative market dominance (or business strength), respectively. Unlike the BCG matrix, the GE/McKinsey model views each axis as a composite of multiple aspects and measures. This makes it much richer than the BCG model[6] and much more realistic in terms of the positioning of SBUs.[7]

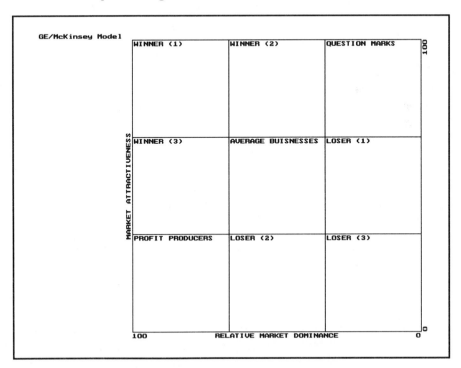

Figure 3.1   GE/McKinsey model.

Though both axes are composed of variables that are both quantitative and nonquantitative, the variables of the Y axis are less, or not at all, controllable by the firm (external factors), whereas those of the X axis are controllable by the firm (internal factors).[8]

Grid

One of the salient features of the GE/McKinsey model is the expansion of the 2×2 grid used in the BCG model to a 3×3 grid. The expansion of the grid allows for a more detailed classification of the SBUs and hence, for more specific strategic possibilities.

On the 3×3 grid, SBUs are plotted as circles on a two-dimensional layout of market attractiveness vs. relative market dominance. Each circle or 'bubble' on the grid represents the total sales of the market (or industry) in which a single SBU operates, while the market share of the SBU within the market is represented by a wedge, as in a pie chart.

Both the external/vertical Y axis and the internal/horizontal X axis are divided into high, medium and low ranges. Thus the grid is composed of nine cells. It should be noted that the range on the X axis is conventionally plotted from high to low, beginning from the left, closest to the Y axis, and moving to the right, away from the Y axis. Hax and Majluf[8] suggest two approaches to determine factor weight: 'general' importance, and 'industry specific' importance. In using the 'general' approach, the manager first assigns a weight to each factor or variable (normalized to 100%) and then numerically grades each variable. The final score is the weighted average of the numerical grades. In using the 'industry specific' approach, the approximate level of each factor for each industry is reached through open discussion by management.

Hosmer[9] points out that the 'higher' ranked SBUs do not necessarily get more funding than 'lower' ranked ones; they are merely arranged on a continuum, divided into three parts: above average, average, and below average, on the two axes.

Cells

The matrix further introduces the following colors and corresponding generic names:

- In the green   Winners
- In the yellow   Profit Producers, Average Businesses, and
                    Question Marks
- In the red   Losers

Winners or In the green

SBUs falling in the three cells in the upper left-hand corner of the matrix are rated as 'in the green' and are given the generic name, Winners. These are SBUs that are 'high' on one dimension, and high or medium on the other.

Rating SBUs as 'in the green', like approaching a green traffic light, means a generally positive attitude (GO) toward investment in the SBU. These SBUs are expected to grow, and in so doing will yield a high future return on investment. The strategic decision regarding investments in the SBUs that fall in the green is 'go' or 'invest and grow.'

For each cell we detail:

- Name of the cell and (its location on the grid).

- Strengths, opportunities, threats, and weaknesses.

- Possible SBU strategies.

Winner 1:

High market attractiveness/high relative market dominance (upper left-hand corner).

Attractive market; the SBU is one of the leaders or the leader in the market. The main threat is possible improvement on the part of a competitor.

Possible strategies: take advantage of success and protect relative advantage through continuing investment.

Winner 2:

High market attractiveness/medium relative market dominance (upper middle box).

Attractive market; the SBU is not a leader in the industry but does not lag very far behind.

Possible strategies: locate weak points and strong points and then invest to improve weak points and/or take advantage of strong points.

Winner 3:

Medium market attractiveness/high relative market dominance (middle left-hand box).

High business strength; moderate industry attractiveness.

Possible strategies:

1. locate most attractive market segments and invest in them;

2. build/improve capability to deal with competitors;

3. growth emphasis on profitability by increased production through increased investment;

4. harvest the business, and invest only to maintain competitive position.

Losers or In the red

Conversely, SBUs falling in the three cells in the lower right- hand corner of the matrix are rated as 'in the red' and called Losers. These are SBUs with at least one low and no high ranking on the X and Y axes.

These SBUs should be approached with readiness to come to an investment standstill, as the red color suggests. They are expected to continue to generate earnings, but no longer warrant additional investment. The strategic decision regarding these losers is 'stop' or severely limit additional investment.

Loser 1:

Medium market attractiveness/low relative market dominance (middle right-hand box).
No special strengths or competitive opportunities; limited attractiveness, little growth, a fairly competitive market.
Possible strategies:

1. locate possibilities of improving position in areas of low risk;

2. develop areas in which the SBU has a clear advantage;

3. harvest areas of current strength;

4. leave.

Loser 2:

Low market attractiveness/medium relative market dominance (middle lower box).
No special strengths or opportunities; unattractive industry or pro-duct–market; SBU is not the leader, but is a viable competitor.
Possible strategies:

1. concentrate investment to decrease risk;

2. protect position of SBU in most profitable segments;

3. leave – sell SBU if price offered is satisfactory.

Loser 3:

Low market attractiveness/low relative market dominance (lower right-hand corner).

No special strengths or opportunities; unattractive industry; SBU lags far behind the leader.
Possible strategies:

1. harvest: manage to obtain current profits;

2. decrease fixed costs and avoid investments;

3. leave – sell SBU at reasonable price (the sooner one is able to leave, the better the chances of a good price for the SBU).

Profit Producers, Average Businesses, and Question Marks or In the yellow

The SBUs falling in the three cells along the remaining lower left to upper right diagonal of the matrix are said to be 'in the yellow' or 'borderline'. These are SBUs with medium or mixed high–low ratings on the X and Y axes. They are either SBUs that are as likely to grow as not (that is, they may or may not have high future ROI) or SBUs with subunits that need individual investment decisions. Thus, in dealing with the SBUs falling in the yellow, the strategic manager should 'slow down', because the decision concerning these SBUs is more complex and needs special attention. Each SBU that falls in the yellow is given its own generic name: Question Mark, Average Business or Profit Producer.

Question Marks:

High market attractiveness/low relative market dominance (upper right-hand corner).
Attractive industry; business lags behind leaders.
Possible strategies:

1. selective building – develop existing strong areas to improve competitive position;

2. locate niches and invest in them;

3. leave – if improvement in competitive position is not forthcoming and the above strategies cannot be applied.

Average Businesses:

Medium market attractiveness/medium relative market dominance (middle box).
No special strengths or opportunities; limited industry attractiveness; SBU is not market leader.
Possible strategies:

1. selective investment in profitable, low-risk market segments;

2. scrutinize existing policies carefully;

3.   develop areas where SBU has clear advantage.

Profit Producers:

Low market attractiveness/high relative market dominance (lower left-hand corner).

Leader in industry; unattractive industry.

Possible strategies:

1.   manage investments to milk short-term profits;

2.   concentrate investment resources in attractive market segments;

3.   protect relative advantage.

Relevant strategic variables

General Electric's original basis of analysis was 40 variables for each SBU. In 1980, they reduced the number to 15. Six of these 15 variables were used to assess market attractiveness (the Y axis) and the remaining 9 were grouped together into two factors, market position and competitive strength, to describe relative market dominance (the X axis).[10] To use the GE/McKinsey model, values for the following variables should be assigned:

Business strength variables (X axis)	Market attractiveness variables (Y axis)
Relative market share	Market growth rate
Market share growth	Product differentiation
Distribution network coverage	Characteristics of competition
Distribution network effectiveness	Relative industry profitability
Caliber of personnel	Customer value
Customer loyalty	Customer brand loyalty
Technology skills	
Patents	
Marketing skills and strength	
Flexibility	

Market growth rate and relative market share were defined in Chapter 2. Following are the definitions of the new strategic variables.

Business Strength Variables

Market share growth (for X axis)

Definition: The ability of the SBU to maintain present market share with present and future marketing and production capacity.

Distribution network coverage

Definition: The number of dealers/agents and distribution locations the SBU maintains in order to supply demand, and bring the product to the customer, quickly and efficiently (for example, spotty coverage of market, partial coverage of relevant segments, full coverage of relevant segments).

Distribution network effectiveness

Definition: The elements comprising effectiveness are the strength of the SBU's existing distribution links with retail and wholesale customers, its reputation in the trade, sales-force skills and its physical distribution network. Also included are capacity and length of the distribution channels.

Caliber of personnel

Definition: The quality of human resources available to the SBU is measured in terms of employee qualifications, experience, formal education, training, and their efficient and effective use of equipment. The caliber of personnel also consists of values and structure that are consistent with SBU strategy.

Customer loyalty

Definition: The extent to which the SBU has secured future purchases of its products by customers who have purchased the product in the past. Loyalty is measured by the probability that a customer buying your brand now will choose your brand rather than the competitor's on his next purchase occasion. Customers may be loyal to a brand *or* to a store. Moreover, what may appear to be loyalty could be no more than habit, indifference, low price or nonviability of other brands. There are hard-core loyals (purchasing pattern: AAAAA), soft-core loyals (pp: AABBAB), shifting loyals (pp: AAABBB), and switchers (pp: ACEBDB). Absence of loyalty to an SBU could be due to the fact that it does not have branded products. This variable measures the general loyalty of the customers to the SBU's branded products.

Technology skills (production)

Definition: The technological sophistication and innovation of the facilities, equipment and personnel; the number of techniques used in the production and service processes and in raw materials procurement, and their novelty, that is, the degree to which the SBU employs state-of-the-art techniques.

Patents

Definition: An SBU may have advantages over competitors by developing/owning/licensing its own technologies or production processes, especially those protected by patents or copyright laws. These advantages are determined by the number of products or production processes protected by patents or copyright laws, and the degree to which the patent rights are actually enforced, as well as by the number of products the SBU sells under license agreements.

Marketing skills and strength

Definition: The marketing function is dependent on skills and strengths in all areas of the marketing mix: market research, new product development and packaging design, the skills and training of the sales force, budget allocated to marketing, advertising and promotion, and awareness on the part of management of the marketing concept, not to mention the size, scope and position in the hierarchy of the marketing department.

Flexibility

Definition: The ability to handle internal changes, at *any functional level* without disrupting the whole system, and to make the switches quickly and cost-effectively. For example, the ability to switch from one type of raw material to another, using the same machinery, means the machinery is flexible. Switching from production of product A in small batches to product B in large batches (quickly and efficiently) means the manufacturing line is flexible. Flexibility is also measured in management decision making, data handling (is the computer system flexible or rigid?), budgets, manpower, and so on.

Market attractiveness variables

Product differentiation

Definition: How willing are customers to pay for quality/branding (for example, standardized products and low margins, commodity, average differentiation, and highly differentiated products; many buyers willing to pay a high price for perceived quality/brand name)?

Characteristics of the competition

Definition:

Toughness: the general number and quality of competitors as perceived by other competitors or potential entrants in terms of financial strength, production and marketing capability, product quality, market shares, profitability and consistency of strategic moves.

Type: concentrated among a small number of strong competitors, or fragmented among many small competitors.

Structure: one leader and followers, or other structures. The profitability of the industry is related to the degree of competition.

Relative industry profitability

Definition: The industry's average profitability is usually measured by return on equity.

Customer value

Definition: In measuring the general attitude of the customers to the industry/product type in terms of price vs. value (utility), and the tendency to buy the same kind of product again, this variable indicates the value the customers attach to the very existence of the industry. It is the satisfaction of the customers with the products of the industry in general, and not of a specific brand or product. (Frozen TV dinners may have more value added for the customer compared to packaged frozen vegetables, which have to be cooked. The frozen TV dinner market may therefore be more attractive than the frozen vegetable market. Similarly, the home video industry may be more attractive than the movie theater industry.)

Customer brand loyalty

Definition: The overall tendency of customers in the market to repurchase the same product in the future from the same supplier is estimated by the customers' emotional attitude toward the available brands, and/or new brands. This 'general' loyalty, as expressed in purchasing habits, is a function of the maturity of the industry.

Use of the model

The main focus of the GE/McKinsey matrix is the balancing of investments. By plotting each SBU on the matrix, a pattern emerges that represents the expected future ROI of each SBU in the portfolio. The GE matrix should be used to display both the present position of the corporation's SBUs and their future position.[11]

The matrix cannot be used to effectively answer the compelling question of how to reshape the portfolio.[12] This is a question that the corporate manager must answer. At most, the model can offer certain strategic guidelines in the form of generic strategies.

In general, the strategy will be to increase resources to SBUs with high market attractiveness and strong relative market dominance. Conversely, SBUs with low market attractiveness and a weak competitive position will have their resource allocations reduced. For SBUs that fall in between, the strategy will be selective.[13] More explicit strategic models have been suggested. For example, Naylor[14] suggests the following presentation of strategies to be adopted for the different SBU positions:

- Winner 1.   Invest

- Winner 2.   Growth

- Winner 3.   Growth

- Question Mark   Earnings

- Average Business   Earnings

- Profit Producer   Earnings

- Loser 1.   Harvest

- Loser 2.   Harvest

- Loser 3.   Divest

Although Naylor's model contains suggestions of broad strategies, it does not answer the question of how to implement them or solve the problems that might arise in their implementation. The manager must be aware of these potential problems. For example, there is the danger that the 'go' orientation toward the Winner SBUs falling within the cells of the upper left-hand corner of the matrix will be translated into overcommitment of investment resources, beyond the level that the company is capable of supporting in the long term. Furthermore, the high return on investment expected from these SBUs will not come about immediately but sometime in the future. Thus, if the company is too winner-oriented, the resources necessary for the short term may be completely drained, leading to cashflow problems.

Care should also be exercised not to place too much emphasis on the SBUs falling along the lower-left to upper-right diagonal. Although some of these SBUs are expected to yield high returns, it should be noted that this is only in the short term. If too much attention is paid to these SBUs, the short-term gain will be high but the subsequent returns will diminish.

To avoid such problems, it is recommended that the first goal be the protection of the SBUs falling along the diagonal, avoiding excessive investment in them. Returns on investment from these SBUs should be reinvested in the winner SBUs. This will shift the emphasis to both the short-term and long-term gains. The second goal should be to transform the

Question Marks into Winners. That is, by investing in selected SBUs with a weak position in a strong market, the manager could help transform them into strong ones.

Another use of the GE matrix is in competitor analysis. A competitor's portfolio may be assessed at different points in time, to help gain an insight into corporate strategies and policies.[15]

One of the main contributions of the GE model was the change in the reward system for managers that it brought in its wake. GE had, up till the introduction of the SBU concept, rewarded its managers identically, on the basis of residual earnings, that is, controllable profits minus charges for corporate capital and corporate services rendered. Switching over to the SBU concept led to a redefining of the compensation schedule for managers, based on long-term goals vs. short-term goals according to the strategies found to be appropriate. The following table shows the emphasis of bonus distribution, according to these definitions:

SBU classification	Current performance (Residual income)	Future performance (Strategy)	Other factors
Winners (Green)	40%	48%	12%
In the yellow	60%	28%	12%
Losers (Red)	72%	16%	12%

Model's assumptions, misuse and critique

Assumptions

Underlying the GE/McKinsey matrix are a number of basic assumptions concerning the SBU, the X and Y axes, and the constituent elements of these axes.

The SBU

Like all other matrix-portfolio models, this model assumes that the strategic business unit is autonomous. Thus, results may not be meaningful if strategic choices for the individual units being analyzed are in some way dependent on the strategic choices for other units.

The X and Y axes

The construction of the X axis (relative market dominance) is based on the assumption of differences in competitive position that express themselves in varying profits among the competitors. Also inherent in this model is the notion that competitive position will deteriorate over time unless new sources of competitive advantage are found, and that it is therefore desirable to classify a business according to future projections and not only according to its present status.[16]

The construction of the Y axis (market attractiveness) is based on the notion that there is a market or industry attractiveness that reflects itself in the average long-term profit potential for all participants.

The constituent elements of the axes

The GE/McKinsey matrix assumes that the choice of factors comprising the axes is valid and that they can be easily identified and properly weighed by the corporate manager. In developing the matrix, McKinsey and Co. also believed that the factors determining market attractiveness and competitive position varied by market and had to be developed for each market separately.[17] In practice, the choice of variables is easily influenced by historical perceptions, performance, individual biases, and survey methods.[18] Moreover, managers may not know how to identify all relevant variables or how to assess the nature of their relationships.[19] Finally, it is difficult to assign weights to variables, because of the dependence among them, and because the appropriate weighting may vary from market to market.[20]

Misuse

The GE/McKinsey model is frequently misused in two ways. First, managers tend to use it as a prescription for strategic decision making. This is a serious mistake as the model is descriptive rather than prescriptive. In other words, the matrix should be used as an aid to decision making rather than a solution to the strategic problem at hand. The role of the matrix is twofold. It describes the present situation of the SBU and it can help in making accurate future projections.

Second, as Day[20] notes, management teams tend to rate a business at an intermediate position on most factors. It seem that when managers use the GE model in a group decision analysis/planning session, the 'medium' range is often used as a compromise for diverging opinions.[21] This of course is misleading and results in averaged-out assessments, rather than pinpointed specific evaluations. Day[22] suggests that this is due either to compromise or to lack of appreciation of the relevant issues. The outcome is a concentration of business ratings in the center of the matrix and a loss of discriminatory power in the analysis. This in turn may lead to undue concern for insignificant differences rather than critical problems.

Critique

As a composite, multivariable model, the GE/McKinsey matrix draws less criticism than the BCG growth-share matrix. The one-variable approach of the BCG limits the analysis of each SBU to only one quantitative variable, whereas the multivariable approach can more realistically describe the SBU, as many variables, including more qualitative assessments, are considered simultaneously.

Criticism of the GE/McKinsey model has nevertheless been directed at the SBU and product–market definitions, the generic strategies and aspects of the matrix (including grid labels, the dimensions, the variables, and the ROI measure).

SBU and product–market definitions

One of the major problems in portfolio analysis, regardless of the specific model the corporate manager has selected, is defining the SBU and product–market (industry) borders. This is problematic owing to the fact that even relatively small shifts in SBU or product–market definitions may, under certain conditions, lead to significant changes in the appearance of the SBUs on the matrix.

The assessment of each item for each SBU and its relative importance (weight) is made by subjective analysis.[23] There is of course the possibility of human bias in deciding on the weights, as well as the possibility of mathematical errors on the quantitive items.[24] Several authors have noted that the GE model is more vulnerable to manipulation than other models which rely on 'hard' data.[25, 26, 27]

Generic strategies

There are three main criticisms of the generic strategies suggested by this model. The first is that they may lead to 'automatic strategies' which are naive. The second criticism is that generic strategies are too simplistic and serve as a substitute for real in-depth analysis. The third criticism is that they tend to stifle creativity.[28] The possibility of investing in a declining industry does not exist in the GE model, which prescribes harvest/divest in a very general manner. In reality, there are situations in which such an investment can bear luscious fruits.[29]

Features of the matrix

Variables

The measures defining the axes are problematic for a number of reasons. First, the choice of factors to be considered may be biased.[30] Second, those factors identified as relevant may be difficult to assess.[31] Third, the allocation of a weight to each measure is particularly difficult since variables are interrelated and since the importance of factors may well vary in relation to specific market characteristics. Fourth, relevant information is lost in calculating composite scores, since two SBUs may have totally reversed positions on the detailed measures and still end up with the same composite score.[32]

Hax and Majluf[33] criticize the quantitative method of weight allocation as being too mechanistic, claiming that the elements involved are not quantifiable. They nonetheless stress the importance of assigning weights to the variables. Fifth, given the tailoring of factors to each industry, comparison across industries is difficult.[34]

Dimensions

It has been claimed that the X and Y axes are not the appropriate dimensions.[34] One of the main shortcomings of the GE model is that it does not contain a specific method of dealing with new SBUs/products in new industries. That is to say, if the industry is new, its attractiveness cannot be readily assessed (or may be underrated by 'normal' measures), and the relative strength of the SBU cannot be accurately assessed because the competitors are not yet known. The SBU could thus be depicted on the GE matrix as a loser when it actually has winner potential, or vice versa. This limitation also exists in other models and was indeed the trigger for the Hofer model (discussed in Chapter 5), which addresses the market evolution stages.[35]

Cell labels

Managers find that the labels commonly assigned to cells are largely irrelevant and that it is often psychologically difficult to conceptualize the entities behind them.[36]

ROI measure

In using return on investment as the measure of future success, risk is ignored.[37] Furthermore, Wensley[38] notes that the focus on ROI may result in little advantage over methods of analysis that focus upon net present value.

Empirical studies

It seems there is very little empirical research to support the GE model. At the same time, many sophisticated consulting firms seem to be using the model. This suggests that the mix of qualitative and quantitative factors has practical uses.[39] Furthermore, many of the ideas behind the GE model have been corroborated by the various analyses which have been done on the PIMS database.[40]

Variations and additions

The original GE planning screen displayed the position of an SBU in one of the nine cells, and used three 'traffic light zones' – red, green or yellow. Later versions used circles to depict either the size (sales) of the SBU or the size of the market, the relative market share being depicted as a pie wedge within the market-size circle. The two basic types of variations of the original model are variations in generic strategies and variations in the factors constituting the X and Y axes.

Variations in generic strategies

There are different variations in generic strategies for the GE/McKinsey model. Day's[41] approach is a composite of matrices from several sources, including Abell and Hammond,[42] Ohmae,[43] and Hichens, Robinson and Wade.[44]

Monieson[45] quoted in Steiner and Miner,[46] goes even further in his description of the GE models by suggesting that each one of the nine cells in the matrix is indicative of the 'natural strategies' to be pursued by occupants of the respective cell.

Variations in variables

Many variables may, under more general or more specific conditions, affect market attractiveness and competitive strength. Thus it is not surprising that many lists have been suggested.[47, 48] For example, in Hayden,[49] Business Strength includes absolute market share, relative market share, market growth, buyer group growth rate, return on investment, cost structure, relative costs, product differentiation, process technology and management skills, while Industry Attractiveness includes size and growth of sales volume, degree of price competition, industry concentration and share balance, industry profitability, the role of technology in the industry, and the effect of possible changes in the sociopolitical factors that impact the industry.

Wind, Mahajan and Swire[50] combined the factors from the GE/McKinsey model with the ROI variables considered in Day's empirically derived PIMS Par Model.

Table 3.1

Generic strategy options

MARKET	Protect position	Invest to build	Build selectively
ATTRACT-IVENESS High	• invest to grow at maximum digestible rate • concentrate effort on maintaining strength	• challenge for leadership • build selectively on strengths • reinforce vulnerable areas	• specialize around limited strengths • seek ways to overcome weaknesses • withdraw if indications of sustainable growth are lacking
	Build selectively	**Selectivity/Manage for earnings**	**Limited expansion or harvest**
Medium	• invest heavily in attractive segments • build up ability to counter competition • emphasize profitability by raising productivity	• protect existing program • concentrate investments in segments where profitability is good and risk is relatively low	• look for ways to expand without high risk; otherwise, minimize investment and rationalize operations
	Protect and refocus	**Manage for earnings**	**Divest**
Low	• manage for current earning • concentrate on attractive segments • defend strengths	• protect position in most profitable segments • upgrade product line • minimize investment	• sell at time that will maximize cash value • cut fixed costs and avoid investment meanwhile
	Strong	**Medium**	**Weak**
		COMPETITIVE POSITION	

Table 3.1 Generic strategy options (*cont.*)

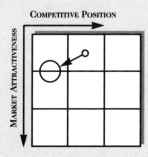

Invest to build: This strategy option is indicated when a highly attractive market offers opportunities for growth that may not be available as the market matures. Significant investments are required to build selectively on strengths and keep up with the rapid growth rates that are typical of these markets.

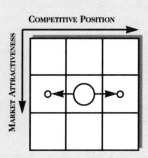

Selectivity/manage for earnings: Here, the indicated option is to strengthen the position of the business in segments where profitability is good or barriers to competitive entry can be maintained, while letting the position erode in segments where costs exceed benefits.

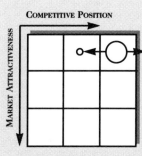

Build selectively or exit: With a weak position in an attractive market, it is usually desirable to look for protected niches in which to specialize. If this is not feasible or the costs/risks are excessive, then an exit should be considered.

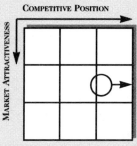

Harvest: This involves exchanging the business position for cash, by minimum investment and rationalization of operations. Selective investment may be made with a view to improving the value of the business if it is to be eventually sold.

Table 3.2

INDUSTRY STRENGTH			
	Premium: invest for growth	**Selective: invest for growth**	**Protect/Refocus: selectively invest for earnings**
High	• provide maximum investment • diversify worldwide • consolidate position • accept moderate near-term profits	• invest heavily in selected segments • share ceiling • seek attractive new segments to apply strength	• defend strengths • refocus to attractive segments • evaluate industry revitalization • monitor for harvest or divestment timing
	Challenge: invest for growth	**Prime: selectively invest for earnings**	**Restructure: harvest or divest**
Medium	• build selectively on strengths • define implications of leadership challenge • avoid vulnerability – fill weaknesses	• segment market • make contingency plans for vulnerability	• provide no unessential commitment • position for divestment *or* • shift to more attractive segment
	Opportunistic: selectively invest for earnings	**Opportunistic: preserve for harvest**	**Harvest or divest**
Low	• ride market • seek niches: specialization •seek opportunity to increase strength (for example, acquisition)	• act to preserve or boost cash-flow • seek opportunistic sale *or* • seek opportunistic rationalization to increase strengths	• exit from market or prune product line • determine timing so as to maximize present value
	High	**Medium**	**Low**
		MARKET ATTRACTIVENESS	

Source: Monieson, D. D.: *Effective Marketing Planning: An Overview*, (Ottawa: The Conference Board of Canada, Executive Bulletin No. 8, 1978)

Table 3.3

This model is patterned after the GE/McKinsey type model using PAR ROI factors. The factors considered in the PIMS Par model have each been identified as belonging to market position or industry attractiveness dimensions.

Market Position	Industry Attractiveness

• Market Share Index
  Market Share
  Relative Market Share
• Relative Product Quality
• Relative Price
• Relative Direct Cost
• Patents re. Process or Products
 	
• Relative Range of Customer Sizes
• Labor Productivity
• Relative Employee Compensation
• Shared Production Facilities
	• Real Market Growth, Long Run
	• Unionization (%)
	• New Products (% of Sales)
	• Research and Development/ Sales
	• Selling–Price Growth Rate
	• Marketing/Sales
	• Purchase Amount by Immed. Cust.
	• % of All End User's Purchases
	• No. Customers = 50% of Sales
	• Products Produced to Order?
	• Industry Concentration
	• Investment Intensity Index Investment/Sales Investment/Value Added
	• Capacity Utilization
	• Gross Book Value of Plant and Equipment/Investment
	• Vertical Integration
	• Investment per Employee
	• Accounting Convention
	• Receivables/Investment
	• Raw Materials and Work-in-Progress/Value Added

Source: pp. 96, Wind, Yoram, Mahajan, Vijay and Swire, D.J (1983) 'An empirical comparison of standardised portfolio models' Journal Of Marketing Vol 47 (spring), pp. 89-99. Full credit to the American Marketing Association.

Day,[51] on the other hand, suggests that a valid approach is to select, from a standard checklist (adapted from Abell and Hammond[52]), those factors that have historically been determinants of industry profitability or relative profitability.

Table 3.4

Factors contributing to market attractiveness and business strength

Attractiveness of Your Business

A. Market Factors
- size (dollars, units)
- size of product market
- market growth rate
- stage in life cycle
- diversity of market (potential for differentiation)
- price elasticity
- bargaining power of customers
- cyclicality/seasonality of demand

B. Economic and Technological Factors
- investment intensity
- nature of investment (facilities, working capital, leases)
- ability to pass through effects of inflation
- industry capacity
- level and maturity of technology utilization
- barriers to entry/exit
- access to raw materials

C. Competitive Factors
- types of competitors
- structure of competition
- substitution threats
- perceived differentiation among competitors

D. Environmental Factors
- regulatory climate
- degree of social acceptance
- human factors such as unionization

Strength of Your Competitive Position

A. Market Position
- relative share of market
- rate of change of share
- variability of share across segments
- perceived differentiation of quality/price/service
- breadth of product
- company image

B. Economic and Technological Position
- relative cost position
- capacity utilization
- technological position
- patented technology, product, or process

C. Capabilities
- management strength and depth
- marketing strength
- distribution system
- labor relations
- relationships with regulators

Hax and Majluf[53] criticize the use of a standardized list of variables. They claim that a prefabricated list will not properly address the specific SBU at hand and suggest that the general list should only be used as a source and a guideline in selecting the specific variables that will address each SBU.

4

The Shell/DPM model

History: Development and use

The Directional Policy Matrix (DPM) was designed in 1975 by the British Dutch-based Shell Chemicals company, as a direct response to the dynamics of the environment at the time: too much crude oil on the market, a drastic decrease in crude oil prices, and low industry profits. In other words, it was the outcome of an immediate need for reliable strategic planning tools in a time of rampant inflation and unpredictable environmental changes, to replace the no longer relevant financial forecasts upon which the oil industry had been basing its strategies. The result indeed was a matrix that relies less on past financial performance and financial projections than previous matrices, such as the GE/McKinsey matrix.

In a vertically integrated corporate array, like that of Shell and other oil companies, decisions must be made on both the allocation of funds to refineries and other business units, and the allocation of crude oil. These complications make it difficult to use portfolio models like the growth-share matrix. Another complication is that the business is constructed along classical lines in that different SBUs share the same production facilities. A multitude of products for different markets all come out of the same refinery, and thus production quantities, costs, and profits are highly interdependent. In addition, the products themselves sometimes compete with each other in the marketplace.[1]

Although the DPM model is similar to the GE/McKinsey matrix – both are expansions of the Boston Consulting Group growth-share matrix – the differences should be noted. In contrast to the 2×2 single-factor BCG matrix, the GE/McKinsey and DPM models are two-dimensional, 3×3 matrices which are based on multiple measures, composed of variables which are both quantitative and qualitative. In both cases, expansion of the BCG grid implies more strategic possibilities. However, in the DPM, the generic strategies are more explicit.[2]

Furthermore, the multivariable approach used by both the GE/McKinsey and DPM matrices is more realistic than the approach used in the BCG matrix to describe the SBUs. At the same time, the DPM tends to be more quantitative in emphasis than the GE/McKinsey model. According to Day,[3] the DPM model is more precise in assessing factor ratings than the GE/McKinsey model.

Finally, whereas the planning focus of the GE/McKinsey model on long-term ROI was a direct reaction to the BCG's narrow planning focus on short-term cash flow, the DPM's planning focus considers both cash flow (short-term) and ROI (long-term).

One of the more salient features of the DPM is that it takes into account SBUs with products in different stages of the life cycle. Thus, the consideration of change over time is an integral feature of the model.

Another significant feature of this matrix is the ability to compare SBUs without having to rely on financial measures. As Hichens, Robinson and Wade[4] point out, models that rely on financial measures run into a number of problems: inflation renders financial forecasts invalid, they are unable to address SBUs in new areas (since no past data are available), and they cannot sufficiently explain the dynamics of individual SBUs and the balance among SBUs.

Despite the DPM's clear advantages, the GE/McKinsey matrix is more popular when a multivariable approach is employed. The popularity of the DPM model has waned in most industries, except for the chemical and other capital-intensive industries.[5]

Planning focus: Cash flow and ROI

As noted above, the DPM has a dual planning focus: short-term cash flow, as in the BCG model, and long-term ROI, as in the GE/McKinsey matrix.

Originally in using the DPM, Shell may have tended more toward the cash-flow focus of the growth-share matrix than the ROI or long-range profitability focus of the GE/Mckinsey model. Hichens *et al.*[6] describe the first use of the DPM as a criterion (along with profit record, other product-related criteria, and judgment) for ranking business sectors when deciding on money, materials, and skilled manpower allocation. They note further that nothing is irrevocable: other layouts may be no less feasible than their 3×3 matrix, and ratings can be plotted in various ways. In their view, however, since one of the cells in the 3×3 matrix carries the suggestion of a strategy of 'cash generation', the DPM can be used to analyze the dynamics and financial balance of the portfolio from the standpoint of cash flow: 'ideally the overall strategy should aim at keeping cash surplus and cash deficit sectors in balance, with a regular input of promising new business coming forward from research to take up the surplus cash generated by the businesses already in or moving into the mature phase.'[6] This thinking suggests a certain carry-over from the BCG. Hichens *et al.* also introduced the concept of a second-order matrix, to be used after the business sectors have been prioritized for purposes of resource allocation. The second-order matrix maps non-product, strategic alternatives in relation to the ranked business sectors.

In using the DPM, the manager's focus is the directing of enough cash from cash-generating SBUs and SBUs on the wane toward investment in SBUs with a high ROI potential.

Use and display of the matrix

Dimensions

As in the other portfolio models, the DPM is a two-dimensional grid, where the X and Y axes represent business strength (competitive position) and industry (product–market) attractiveness, respectively. More specifically, the X axis refers to the competence of the SBU or its ability to take advantage of opportunities in the sector in which it is located. This axis is the *specific* measurement of the SBU's relative competitiveness within its industry.

The Y axis refers to the attractiveness of the sector in which the SBU is operating. This axis is thus the *general* measurement of the industry's health and future prospects.

In the DPM, the names given to the axes are the 'company's competitive capabilities' for the X axis and the 'business sector prospects' for the Y axis.[6]

As mentioned earlier, the DPM's X and Y axes are multifactor composites, and thus they are broader-based than BCG's single-factor dimensions.

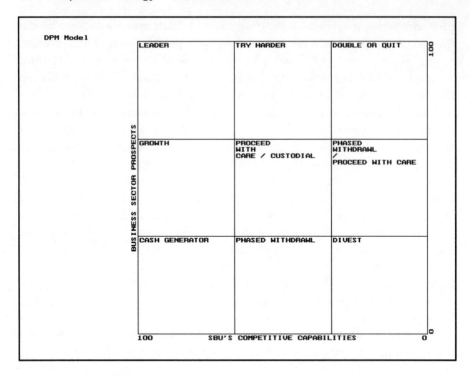

Figure 4.1 DPM model.

Cells[6, 7]

The division of the DPM into a 3×3 grid results in nine cells, each with its own specific strategy, as described below.

For each cell we detail:

- Name of the cell (and its location on the grid).
- Strengths, opportunities, threats, and weaknesses.
- Possible SBU strategies.

Leader:

The industry is attractive and the business strong (upper left-hand cell). This is a more definitive description of the BCG's Star concept.

The SBU is the leader in an attractive industry; the potential market is large, and growth rate is high; no weaknesses or immediate threats.

Possible strategies: invest while the industry continues to grow, in order to defend leadership; large investments are necessary (more than can be internally provided by SBUs falling into this cell); continue to invest, trading current cash flow for future profits.

Growth:

The industry is moderately attractive and the business strong (middle left-hand cell); between the BCG's Star and Cash Cow.

The SBU is one of the leaders, in a mature, moderately growing or stable market with good margins and no other dominant competitor.

Possible strategies: maintenance of position; can provide necessary finances and has excess cash to finance other SBUs in portfolio.

Cash Generator:

The industry is unattractive and the business strong (lower left-hand cell); similar to the BCG's Cash Cow.

The SBU is one of the leaders, if not the leader; the market is stable or declining, industry profit margins have eroded, but there is little threat from competitors, and company productivity is high and costs are low.

Possible strategies: SBUs falling into this cell are the main source of funds in the corporate portfolio; since no future development is expected, the strategy is one of little investment and maximum positive cash flow.

Try Harder:

The industry is attractive and the business strength average (upper middle cell); between the BCG's Star and Problem Child.

As market share, product quality, reputation, and so on, are fairly high (similar to or not much below industry leader), the SBU could turn into a leader if resources are properly invested. Cost disadvantages (experience-curve and scale effects) must be considered before strategic initiative is undertaken.

Possible strategies: invest, if the SBU is worth investing in, making the necessary detailed analysis; large investments would be necessary to move this SBU into the Leader position; an SBU is considered worthy of investment if it can attain a distinct competitive advantage.[8] The investment necessary will be larger than the cash expected to be generated from this SBU and additional investment may be required for an extended fight over market share.

Proceed with Care or Custodial:

The industry is moderately attractive and the business strength average (middle cell).

There are no special strengths or opportunities; the market is growing slowly, stable or slowly declining, and industry profit margins are average. The SBU has some strengths and some weaknesses, but is definitely behind the industry leader.

Possible strategies: invest carefully and in small amounts, ensure that feedback is quick, and make careful analysis.

Phased Withdrawal:

The industry is unattractive and the business strength average (lower middle cell).

There are no special strengths and virtually no opportunities; the market is unattractive (low profit margins, possibly overcapacity, high capital intensity) and declining.

Possible strategies: since it is unlikely that SBUs falling into this cell will provide significant earnings, the suggested strategy is not to develop or invest but rather to convert physical assets and market position into cash, and use resources for more attractive prospects elsewhere.

Double or Quit:

The industry is attractive and the business weak (upper right-hand cell); comparable to Problem Child in the BCG.

The SBU is in a weak competitive position in an attractive market.

Possible strategies: invest or quit. Since a broad-front effort to enhance the competitive position of SBUs falling into this cell would entail large and risky investment, it should be undertaken only after very careful analysis. If it has been established that the SBU is capable of competing for the leadership position, then the strategy is 'Double'. Otherwise, the strategy according to Harvey[9] should be 'Quit'. Only some SBUs should receive double investment, the rest should quit. One other strategy, which may be a feasible alternative in less homogeneous markets, is 'redefine'. If the firm can define a niche where it will be leader and later defend it against competitor attacks, this could be a lower-risk alternative.

Phased Withdrawal/Proceed with Care:

The industry is moderately attractive and the business position weak (middle right-hand cell).

There are no special strengths and limited opportunities; the SBU is in a weak business position, and is unlikely to earn significant amounts of cash.

Possible strategies: no further investment, manage for cash flow and maintain position as long as it is profitable, gradually divest.

Divest:

The industry is unattractive and the business position weak (lower right-hand cell); this is a more definitive description of the BCG's Dog.

There are no special strengths or opportunities; the SBU is in a weak business position in a weak market.

Possible strategies: since SBUs falling into this cell lose money on average, every effort should be made to keep them out, by maintaining a balanced portfolio. Should an SBU still find itself in this cell, the strategy is to divest, as rapidly as possible.

Relevant strategic variables

To use the DPM/Shell model, values for the following variables should be assigned:

Business strength variables (X axis)	Market attractiveness variables (Y axis)
Relative market share	Market growth rate
Distribution network coverage	Relative industry profitability
Distribution network effectiveness	Customer value
Technology skills	Customer brand loyalty
Product line breadth and depth	Competitive lead time
Facilities and location	Relative stability of industry profitability
Production efficiency	
Experience-curve	Technological barriers to entry
Feedstock	Customer/manufacturer bargaining power
Product quality	Supplier bargaining power
Research and development	Impact of government regulations
Economies of scale	Customer/manufacturer bargaining power
After-sales service	
	Supplier bargaining power
	Impact of government regulations
	Utilization of industry capacity
	Product substitutability
	Generation of after-sales business
	Industry's capacity for response
	Industry image

Following are the definitions and measurements of the new variables not defined in the previous chapters.

Business strength variables

Product line breadth and depth

Definition: The relative number and diversity of the business unit's products: the breadth of the product line is the number of different product lines (for example, shampoo, hand and body soaps, hand and body lotion); the depth of the product line is the number of separate items and sizes of products within a specific line (for example, shampoo for regular hair 100cc, shampoo for regular hair 500 cc, shampoo for dry hair 100 cc).

Facilities and location

Definition: The advantage the SBU may have in owning many and/or large and/or new production facilities with new and modern equipment and production techniques, in choice locations.

Production efficiency

Definition: The present production capacity of the SBU, and the extent to which it is used efficiently and effectively, is measured by comparing the SBU to itself (capacity utilization) and by comparing it to competitors in the industry (total potential capacity). Production capacity is also measured by the breadth and depth of product lines.

Experience-curve

Definition: The experience-curve illustrates the advantages of lower production, distribution and selling costs of a particular product owing to accumulated experience.

The concept states that the total constant-dollar-per-unit cost of producing, distributing, and selling a particular product will decline by a constant percentage (usually between 10 and 30 percent) with every doubling of the accumulated production volume in units. Thus the experience-curve effect is very important in fast-growing markets, which accumulate experience very quickly. The following chain is assumed for the SBU:

- High accumulated volume, implies

- Low unit cost, implies

- High profitability.

Experience-curve effects can be measured at all stages of the value-added chain. The user is not required to calculate the experience-curve slope for each link of the chain, but rather to make a *subjective assessment* of the overall experience of the SBU by separate factors at each link, relative to other competitors. The factors are: personal learning of a task; standardization of a task performed many times; product and process improvements; methods and system rationalization – mainly by introducing automation and computerization, both of which require reaching a certain volume (an expensive process); economies of scale.

Feedstock (raw material accessibility and cost)

Definition: The term feedstock encompasses the advantage the SBU might have in acquiring raw materials (or components or subsystems) of high quality, with fast delivery time, and at cheap prices, owing to good relationships with suppliers, or high bargaining power over these suppliers. Raw materials costs are compared to the costs of other competitors.

Product quality

Definition: Relative product quality is defined by subjective and objective terms.
Subjective: The relative quality as it is perceived by the customer, based on past experience, general image, and brand perception.
Objective: The relative quality of the raw materials used, special features, specifications, durability, reliability, zero returns, and so on.

Research and development

Definition: This is a measure of R&D staff skills in terms of innovation, creativity, simplicity, quality, reliability, budgeting, and so on. It is the ability of the SBU to access outside sources of research and engineering and/or license its R&D skills to others. It is also determined by the relative amount of new products designed and brought to the market.

Economies of scale

Definition: The SBU may gain advantages by producing large batches, with minimal set-up time between batches; cost advantages may also be gained by large procurement orders, allowing for reductions from suppliers, or the simultaneous delivery of large quantities to several customers.

After-sales service

Definition: The SBU's ability to maintain quick and efficient after-sales service, be it repairs and maintenance, guarantee and warranty services, or customer follow-up for additional sales, as well as the size and scope of the service department and service network.

Market attractiveness variables

Competitive lead times

Definition: The attractiveness of the market to new competitors if and when a new product appears: are lead times long enough to deter new competitors? Definitions of attractiveness here relate to *existing* competitors.

Relative stability of industry profitability

Definition: The ability of the industry to maintain (high) profits over a long period, despite market changes such as fluctuating demand, entrance of new competitors, increased costs, overcapacity, and so on, cannot be assessed for *new* industries.

Technological barriers to entry
(from the point of view of the existing manufacturers)

Definition: The degree to which technology represents a barrier to market entry: Is technology available to all or to just a few manufacturers? Is it limited (patented) or common knowledge? Is it enforced by regulation, by government or by the developers of the technology? To what degree is new technology required by the industry's customers?

Customer/manufacturer bargaining power

Definition: The bargaining power balance is determined by the ratio of customers to manufacturers. A balance in favor of the customers may also be a result of one or more of the following: large purchase quantities; the existence of qualified alternative sources; low transaction costs; low switching costs (to other suppliers); the possibility of threatening with backward integration. An attractive market from the point of view of the manufacturer is one with low customer bargaining power.

Supplier bargaining power or supplier/manufacturer bargaining balance

Definition: The balance will swing depending on the changes to be made in a product, and the amount of money and learning time involved in changing suppliers of raw materials/components, as well as the degree to which the formulation (specifications) of the product or the machinery for production must be changed when suppliers are changed. The two titles constitute the single variable described by Porter:[10] power of suppliers. The more the SBU is dependent on compatibility with one specific supplier, the greater the bargaining power of the supplier *vis-à-vis* the SBU. An attractive market will therefore be one in which components and parts are standardized and interchangeable.

Impact of government regulations

Definition: The extent to which regulatory agencies, legislative bodies and environmental control associations are involved in the industry and can influence standards for production processes, products, waste removal, work security and safety, labor laws, energy consumption, import quotas, and so on. Examples of tightly controlled industries are pharmaceuticals and military equipment.

Utilization of industry capacity

Definition: Examples are industry at undercapacity most of the time, average capacity utilization, varies with cycles, and industry close to capacity most of the time.

Product substitutability

Definition: The threat created by the variety of products or services (new or existing) that can perform the same function or satisfy the same need as the SBU's product and the ease with which the customer can switch.

High substitutability exists when customer needs are easily filled by other products/services. On the other hand, low or zero substitutability exists when there are no reasonable substitutes from the customer's viewpoint.

Generation of after-sales business

Definition: The inherent ability of the industry to create after-sales business, such as another sale, the sale of a complementary product, or a guarantee contract.

Industry's capacity for response to sudden demand

Definition: The availability of all input requirements, such as raw materials, components and subsystems, and the ability of the industry's suppliers to supply large quantities if demand rises, are collectively defined as the industry's feedstock and lead time.

Industry image

Definition: The industry's general image is its image as perceived by customers, labor, other stakeholders and the general public, in terms of social responsibility, labor relations, environmental issues and overall contribution to society.

Use of the model

In common with other portfolio models, the DPM is descriptive and prescriptive. That is, the manager may use the model both to describe the SBUs' actual (or expected) position, according to the relevant variables, and to prescribe strategies. The prescribed strategies should, however, be viewed with caution. The model is meant to act as an aid and not as a replacement for in-depth decision making.

Portfolio models, including the DPM, may be used for plotting the corporation's portfolio, a competitor's portfolio, or both. The last-mentioned plot, of the corporation's portfolio in juxtaposition to that of a competitor, provides a better overview of a complex situation. Since the model is a simplified, graphic representation, the manager will be better able to envisage the effect of any strategic decision made by the corporation in relation to the competitor, and vice versa.

Portfolio models may also be used in describing portfolios or prescribing strategies over time. Since each plot represents a specific point in time, the manager wishing to see changes over time needs only to plug in data for each period and compare the results. It should be noted that the DPM is a particularly effective portfolio model for visualizing development and change over time, since it does not rely on financial, that is, historical data. Thus, the DPM can be used to evaluate portfolios even at the planning stage.

In a well-managed portfolio, the optimal movement of the SBUs can be described according to the SBU life-cycle stage and cash flow.

SBU life cycle

Optimal movement: from the upper right to lower left cells (Double or Quit – Try Harder – Leader – Growth – Cash Generator – Phased Withdrawal – (Divest))

McNamee[11] stresses that the vertical movement on the matrix is not in the company's control, whereas the horizontal movement is in the company's control, since it is affected by the company's strategies.

The stages of the movement are as follows:

- **Double or Quit:**
  A new SBU which is in need of R&D activity is chosen as part of the portfolio. The market is attractive but because the SBU is new, its competitive position is low. The strategy is investment.

- **Try Harder:**
  With investment, the SBU's position improves, thereby causing a horizontal movement to the left of the matrix. The market continues to grow and the strategy is to continue to invest.

- **Leader:**
  With continued investment, the SBU's position continues to improve, resulting in further horizontal movement to the left. The market continues to grow and the manager continues to invest.

- **Growth:**
  Eventually market growth slows down. This causes vertical downward movement of the SBU. The SBU grows at the same rate as the market.

- **Cash Generator:**
  The market matures and growth is stopped, causing further vertical movement downward. The strategy is to invest only at the rate necessary to maintain position, and manage for cash flow.

- **Phased Withdrawal (Divest) :**
  The market moves toward decline, industry profitability has eroded, and the SBU's position also begins to decline, since recent investment in it has been very limited.

Further investment in this SBU is totally halted, and the decision may be to divest.

Cash flow

Optimal movement: from the lower left to upper right cells. That is, the cash that is generated from the Cash Generator and Phased Withdrawal is used to fund the SBUs requiring funding – that is, selected Double or Quit and all Try Harder.

McNamee[11] claims that management's task is to try to create both an internal and external strategic balance.

The internal strategic balance entails balancing SBUs in relation to their life-cycle stages as well as creating a financial balance. Balancing SBUs according to the product life cycle ensures that enough of them will always be at the mature stage of the life cycle to generate adequate funding to return to stockholders, finance new SBUs and maintain SBUs in need of cash. A financial balance means that the cash-generating SBUs have sales that are large enough to finance cash-consuming SBUs.

For external strategic balance, the SBUs must be spread out over different industries so that risk is minimized.

Active management of the portfolio, then, consists of increasing the competitive advantage of the SBU while simultaneously pruning the portfolio of SBUs which are no longer in effective positions on the matrix.

Plotting several major multi-industry rivals on the same matrix over a period of time can add valuable insight into the patterns of investment and divestment of these rivals. This may help in indicating vulnerable SBUs within one's own corporation, or SBUs that require special attention. The major drawback of this type of incremental analysis is that rival SBUs may change hands abruptly through acquisition and divestment, altering the power structure of the rivalry.[12]

Model's assumptions, misuse, and critique

Assumptions

The basic assumption is that composite variables are necessary to describe the axes of the matrix. Profitability prospects are determined by market growth rate, market quality, industry inputs (availability of raw materials and labor in the industry), and environmental aspects. Competitive capabilities are determined by market position, production capability, and product R&D.[13]

Most of the basic assumptions made in the DPM are similar to those of the GE/McKinsey matrix. Like the GE/McKinsey model, the DPM makes assumptions regarding the SBU, the axes, and the variables.

SBU assumption

As in all portfolio models, the DPM assumes that the SBU is an autonomous unit.

Assumptions regarding the X and Y axes

Underlying the X axis (the company's competitive capabilities) is the assumption that the market is oligopolistic, since the recommended strategy for an SBU with a weak competitive position (because of a negligible market share, low quality, lackluster reputation, and so on) is instant or phased withdrawal from the market.

A further assumption is that there is a gap in competitive position which will widen if a new source of competitive advantage is not found.

The Y axis (the business sector's prospects) assumes the existence of an 'industry attractiveness', which is the long-term profit potential for all the members in that industry.

Assumptions regarding the variables

As in the GE/McKinsey matrix, the DPM assumes that the choice of variables is objective and that they are easy to identify and weigh.

Misuse

The two main types of misuse of the DPM are the same as for the GE/McKinsey model. First, managers tend to follow the generic strategies too literally. Instead of carefully analyzing the portfolio under examination and using the suggested strategies as guidelines, managers often use them as absolute prescriptions.

Second, as noted by Day,[14] there is a tendency among management teams to rate a business at an intermediate position on most factors. The result is that most SBUs are plotted as falling in the center of the matrix.

As in other portfolio matrix models based on relative market position, it is extremely important to define the market/industry in which the SBU operates accurately, in order to assess both market attractiveness and relative strength. Misdefining the market leads to erroneous strategies.[15]

Critique

One of the main benefits of the DPM is that it solves the problems of integrating qualitative and quantitative variables into a single portfolio model.[16] Unlike the BCG matrix, it is not totally dependent on the statistical link between market share and profitability.

The use of detailed measures, especially in a planning context, has the shortcoming of requiring more subjective assessments. On the other hand, it is valuable for executives in defining the strategic variables that play an important role in their particular industry.

Despite the popularity of the DPM, particularly with oil and other capital-intensive companies, the manager should be aware of its drawbacks, most of which are similar to those of the GE/McKinsey matrix.

SBU and product–market definition

One of the main problems of all corporate portfolio models lies in determining how broad the SBU and product–market definition should be. All of the models are sensitive to relatively small changes in SBU or product–market definitions.

The matrix

Variables

1. The choice of variables is often biased.[17]

2. There are no criteria for deciding whether using a small or large number of factors would be preferable in the analysis.[18]

3. It is difficult to assess which variables are significant.[19]

4. Allocation of weights to variables in constructing the dimensions is problematic for several reasons, which vary somewhat according to the method used:

    (a) The qualitative method, where weight allocation is determined by a group, may be affected by the usual problems associated with group decision making, such as 'groupthink'.

    (b) The quantitative method is criticized by Hax and Majluf[20] as being too mechanistic, considering that the entity being evaluated is really more qualitative in nature than quantitative.

    (c) If we decide to give SBUs the same measure weights, the analysis becomes overgeneralized. On the other hand, the assignment of different measure weights to SBUs makes them noncomparable.[21]

   (d) Measures are interrelated.

   (e) Importance of measures for SBU success varies in relation to the specific market.

   (f) Determining the level of each dimension as a weighted average of the component measures leads to loss of information.[22]

5.   It is difficult to make a comparison across industries since component measures should be tailored to each industry.[23]

The model is often criticized for being too costly. The analysis of each relevant measure and its weight allocation is expensive in terms of human resources, particularly when the group decision-making method is used.

Like the GE/McKinsey model, the DPM has been criticized for allowing for too much subjectivity in management's choice of measures. This problem is even more serious in the case of the DPM since it aspires to be more 'objective and precise' in its approach.

The DPM purports to include risk in the analysis. However, it has been criticized for not consistently or sufficiently addressing this factor. Hussey[24] claims that while the DPM includes risk under 'environmental aspects', the environmental aspects themselves are not used consistently in the analysis, and in any case, they do not fully deal with the question of risk. Because of the importance he attached to this factor, Hussey later, when he was associated with the Rolls-Royce company, expanded the DPM to include environmental risk. His adaptation of the DPM model is known as the Risk Matrix and will be discussed later.

Adaptations and variations

The original DPM, as developed by the British Dutch-based Shell Chemicals company, is presently being used in oil and capital-intensive companies, and adaptations of it have been used in other companies. The adaptations of the DPM include variations in the factors which constitute the X and Y axes and in the method of weight allocation. The DPM has also been extended to include additional, second-order matrices. This allows for further segmentation by the addition of variables important for specific markets. For example, Channon[25] notes a matrix that has business attractiveness on one axis and corporate geographic priorities on the other.

Weiss and Tallett[26] state that the basic concepts of grids for multi-business companies are not radically different from each other. Using a combination of the ideas of the BCG and subsequent matrices, they depict 'today's zoo', describing it as consisting of Infants, Wildcats, Stars, Cash Cows, Dogs, War Horses and Dodos.

There are also variations in the DPM concerning the method of rating of the variables. The original method of assigning ratings to variables in the model has been described by Hichens, Robinson and Wade.[27] In the original method, the rating is according to 'stars' (1 to 5) that are translated into corresponding 'weights' (1 star = 0 weight, 5 stars = 4 weight, with 0 and 4 having the least and most weights respectively). The ratings of variables describing the X axis are added together, as are the ratings of the Y variables. The final X and Y scores constitute the SBU's location on the matrix.

A variation of the Hichens et al.[27] rating and weighting method is described by McNamee.[28] In McNamee's method, the allocation is according to 'importance' and 'strength' rather than stars and weights. Importance has a scale of 0–5, with 0 representing 'no importance', 3 representing 'average importance', and 5 representing 'critical importance'. Strength is on a scale from –5 to +5, with –5 as a factor with the strongest possible negative effect, 0 as a factor that has a neutral impact on the company, and +5 as a factor with the strongest possible positive impact. The overall score of each factor is determined by multiplying importance by strength. As in the Hichens et al.[29] model, the sum of scores on the variables describing the X and Y axes is the final score determining the SBU's position on the matrix.

Wind and Mahajan,[30] give a comprehensive list of variables that make up the two composite variables of the DPM: the prospects for sector profitability and the company's competitive capabilities. The factors are detailed below.

The prospects for sector profitability	The company's competitive capabilities
Industry growth	Market share *
Share of the four largest firms	Relative market share
The percentage of customers that generate 50% of sales	Relative quality *
	Relative price *
Investment/sales *	R&D/sales
Fixed capital intensity *	Marketing/sales
Vertical integration *	
Value-added per employee ±	
Capacity utilization	

The variables marked with an asterisk are additions to the original Shell DPM model, as defined by Wind and Mahajan.

Other lists include variables such as:

Market growth rate	Vulnerability to inflation
Stability of demand	Relative market share
Availability of resources	Product/service quality
Product and process volatility	Reputation
Number of customers and suppliers	Favorable access to resources
	R&D strength
Ease of entry	Relative productivity and costs
Government support/regulation	Community and government relations
Gross and net margins	

The product–market evolution portfolio model

History: Development and use

The product–market evolution matrix followed the BCG and the GE matrices. The initiative for this third model came from Charles W. Hofer, a leading authority on business policy, who felt that neither the BCG nor the GE model utilized the appropriate measures for analyzing new businesses in new markets, that is, those businesses just beginning to grow.

Hofer first introduced the model in his *Conceptual Constructs for Formulating Corporate and Business Strategies.*[1] Later it was included in his *Strategy Formulation: Analytical Concepts,*[2] co-authored with Dan Schendel. Professor Schendel, of Purdue University, is also the founder of the Strategic Management Association and editor of the *Strategic Management Journal.*

The product–market evolution matrix presented a new outlook on balancing portfolios: in addition to the assorted strategies assigned to each

SBU, different performance criteria for each stage of the life cycle are introduced.[3]

Another factor that triggered the development of this portfolio matrix was the fact that up to 1978 very few of the researchers in the area had made the distinction between corporate-level strategy and business-level strategy. The new model clearly makes this distinction.

Hofer and Schendel discuss three separate levels of strategy formulation: the corporate level, the business level and the functional level. In general, they address five principles in the strategy formulation process:

- The separation of goal-formulation and strategy-formulation processes.

- The division of strategy formulation into two levels: corporate and business.

- The inclusion of social and political analyses in the process.

- The prime necessity of contingency planning.

- The exclusion of budgeting and implementation planning from the strategy-formulation process.

Another major contribution of Hofer and Schendel is their comprehensive discussion on defining and separating the various SBUs within a corporation. However, their approach is not widely used.[4]

The planning focus: Managing the life cycle

The planning focus concentrates on positioning existing SBUs within the product–market evolution matrix, establishing an ideal future portfolio on the matrix, and identifying strategies for achieving the ideal portfolio. This can be done either by acquiring or selling SBUs and/or by changing or enhancing the strategies of current SBUs.

The position of each SBU is defined according to the maturity of its market and its strength relative to the competition. Different strategies at the business level can be set according to the life-cycle stage of the SBU's product–market.

In their model, Hofer and Schendel offer three types of ideal portfolios at the corporate level: a growth portfolio, a profit portfolio, and a balanced portfolio. Corporations may strive to achieve one of these three 'ideal' portfolios, whose objectives, goals, and required resource levels are different, and lead the corporation to different future scenarios. A growth portfolio has many SBUs at the early stages of the life cycle. Its goals emphasize the long term, and it may run into cash-flow problems in the short term. A profit portfolio has many SBUs in the mature stage, and profit is a short-term goal. This type of portfolio may encounter problems in the future, when the product–markets begin to decline. A balanced portfolio has, as its name implies, a balanced mix of SBUs at all stages. In all three of these 'ideal' portfolios the SBUs are strong compared to the competition. An ideal portfolio does not include average or weak SBUs.

Use and display of the matrix

Dimensions

Y Axis: Product–Market Stage of Evolution

This axis depicts the stage of evolution of the total market/industry relevant to the given SBU. The original Hofer–Schendel model includes five main categories: market development, growth, shakeout, maturity and saturation. Saturation is further divided into three sub-stages – saturation, decline, and petrification. In the following discussion, the Y axis of the Hofer–Schendel model is composed of five stages: development, growth, shakeout, maturity, and decline.

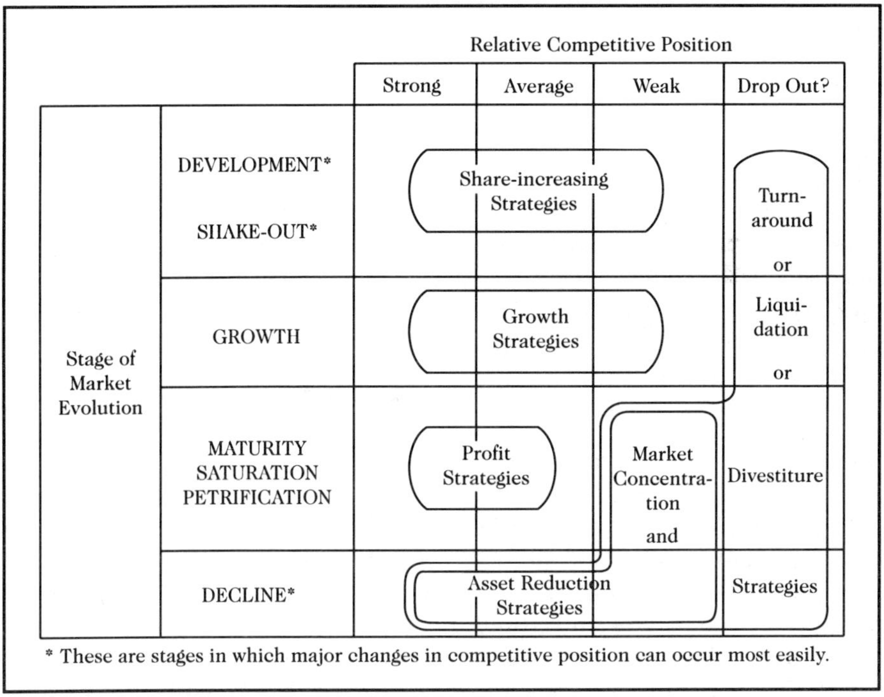

Figure 5.1 Hofer matrix model.

Reprinted by permission from p. 104 of *Strategy Formulation Analytical Concepts* by Hofer, C.W. and D. Schendel; Copyright © 1978 by West Publishing Company. All rights reserved.

X Axis: Relative competitive position

This axis displays the relative competitive position of the SBU within its industry. It is divided into three categories: Strong, Average, Weak. The original model included a fourth competitive position called 'Drop Out?'. Since this is a clear failure position, this book drops this category as a competitive position worthy of separate analysis, and relates to it as part of the liquidation strategy.[5]

Grid

The matrix is in 5×3 form, the horizontal (X) axis displaying the business strength from left to right (strong to weak) and the vertical (Y) axis displaying the life cycle from top to bottom (development at the top and decline at the bottom).

From the position of the SBU within the matrix, the generic strategy recommended for the SBU may be inferred. In Figure 5.1 the generic strategies are superimposed upon the matrix. As one can see, a single generic strategy may be suitable for more than one matrix cell.

The following is a discussion of the six generic strategies.

Share-increasing strategies

The fundamental purpose of share-increasing strategies is to significantly and permanently increase the market share of the relevant business. Implementing these strategies requires a higher investment level than the industry average. Just to keep abreast, the SBU will need to increase its current sales by at least the market growth rate, which may reach 50% or more. If the SBU is in an average or weak competitive position, and is to reach a position of strength, the increase will have to be of the order of 100–150% or even more. Significant increases in market share are usually accomplished by means of horizontal mergers, or by developing a unique competitive advantage. In each stage of the product–market evolution, different opportunities for competitive advantage may be feasible. In the development stage, competitive advantage may be achieved through product design, product positioning, or product quality. In the shakeout stage, it may be achieved through product features, market segmentation, pricing, service improvements or effective distribution. Other stages offer fewer opportunities: competitive advantages are achieved mainly through mistakes of the leader or by taking advantage of sudden breakthroughs in technology.

Growth strategies

The purpose of these strategies is to maintain a competitive position in rapidly growing markets. The absolute level of investment is high, but relative to the industry it is average. Markets grow rapidly during the early stages, and the SBU thus requires substantial resources to keep pace; it needs, moreover, to consolidate its competitive advantages before the shakeout stage, if it is not to be 'shaken out'. One of the main pitfalls of these strategies is that whereas SBUs may spend the resources, they do not always succeed in achieving a viable competitive position.

Profit strategies

In the maturity stage of the life cycle, when competition starts to stabilize and the rate of market growth slows down, the SBU's prime goal should shift from growth to profitability. Investment should be kept at maintenance levels and the return on existing resources and skills should be maximized. Profitability can be achieved through skillful market segmentation and the efficient utilization of existing assets. In order to increase the efficiency of resource utilization, the SBU should identify areas where expenses can be cut, revenues increased, and potential synergies exploited. A successfully developed and implemented profit strategy should result in positive, high cash throw-off, to be invested in growing businesses. Profits may also be reinvested in the SBU but only when it is obvious that the leader has fallen asleep, or the SBU (or its industry) is on the verge of a technological breakthrough. The environment should be monitored for these trends.

Market concentration and asset reduction strategies

The purpose of these strategies is to redefine the scope and level of asset deployment in order to improve short-term profits, and to enhance long-term opportunities. This is accomplished by the realignment of resources and skills to correspond to the new market segments the business intends to serve. Some of the business' assets are shut down, while moderate investments are made to refocus the remaining assets. This usually means a narrower scope and a lower level of investment in the SBU.

In the maturity and saturation stages, if the SBU has a 15% market share (relative to the leader) it should redefine its market, confining it to the segments in which its competitive advantage is greatest. If the SBU has less than a 5% market share, it can concentrate on a small defensible niche, acquire several similar firms in order to achieve a 15% market share, sell out to another corporation, or liquidate the SBU. Acquiring 15% or selling out are not usually feasible by late maturity and saturation. In some cases it is wise to locate a niche that is not likely to disappear completely, and concentrate on it. The final size of the remaining segment and the active competitors should be fully assessed before the decision to concentrate on the segment is taken.

Turnaround strategies

The purpose of these strategies is to stop the process of declining sales as quickly as possible. Sometimes they require the investment of capital and resources, and in other instances they are self-financing. These strategies should be applied only to those SBUs that have a long-run profitability potential, and that will bring in more value as an ongoing concern than as a liquidated asset. The answer to this lies in assessing the attractiveness of the market. Before adopting a turnaround strategy it is necessary to analyze the reason for the decline: was it due to a faulty previous strategy or to poor strategy implementation? Once a turnaround is decided on, the SBU has four alternatives: increase revenues; decrease costs; reduce assets; or any combination of the three.

Liquidation and divestiture strategies

The goal is to generate as much (positive) cash as possible while gradually or precipitously withdrawing from the business. Hofer and Schendel reason that there is no profit in trying to bolster a weak position in an unattractive market.

Liquidation and divestiture strategies should be implemented while the SBU still has some influence or negotiating power, otherwise it will not be 'milkable'. The strategy could include selling idle equipment, dropping customers with long collection periods and pruning products with lower than average margins and high inventory requirements. Even if withdrawal benefits the competition it is more important to exit the market and focus resources on better opportunities.

Relevant strategic variables

To use the product–market evolution portfolio matrix, values for the following variables should be assigned. The following are the definitions and measurements of the new variables not defined in the previous chapters.

Business-strength variables

Key account advantage

Definition: A key account has the advantage of special market relations such as being a supplier to an internationally renowned company like IBM or Marks & Spencer. The advantages of key accounts include customer commitment and long-term contracts. In return, the SBU may have to provide tailor-made products or promise exclusive rights.

Business-strength variables (X axis)	Life-cycle stage variables (Y axis)
Relative market share	Life-cycle stage
Market share growth	Market growth rate
Distribution network coverage	Change in market growth
Distribution network effectiveness	Rate of technological change in product
Product-line breadth and depth	
Facilities and location	Rate of technological change in process
Production efficiency	
Experience-curve	Market segmentation
Feedstock	Major functional concern
Product quality	
R&D	
Key account advantage	
Price competitiveness	
Promotional strength	
Vertical integration	
General image	

Price competitiveness

Definition: The relative attractiveness of the SBU's *current* prices as perceived by the customer compared to other competitors' prices, and the *ability* of the SBU to offer prices that are perceived by the customer as more attractive than those of competitors, by means of discounts, rebates, sales, low interest, special events, and so on.

Promotional strength

Definition: The level and impact of the SBU's advertising and promotion on its sales. Industry norms of advertising must be considered here.

Vertical integration (value-added)

Definition: The extent to which all activities of the value-added chain are owned and performed in-house or the degree of ownership and control of the SBU on the various stages of its operations from production of raw material to ownership of retail outlets. Value-added is the addition to the value of the components as they are combined to form a product, and the value added to the finished product by bringing it to the market place.

Higher-value added is associated with potentially higher profits. Return on value-added tends to be higher for businesses with high engineering content, unique and differentiated products, or highly skilled labor.[6]

Value-added may be measured at the following stages: raw material, intermediate manufacturing, assembly, distribution and retail, if – of course – the SBU performs all of these functions. Value-added is different at each stage of the chain, it is different for dissimilar industries, and for different competitors, depending on the length of the value-added chain (one may do retailing, while the other does not). The value-added of the SBU is compared to that of its competitors within the industry and is calculated by: the selling price of the product less the costs of materials, sub-products and supplies that were employed in producing the product *and* bringing it to the customer.

General image

Definition: The SBU's general image is its image as perceived by competitors, customers and other stakeholders, in terms of business strength, product quality, recognized brand names, quality of operations, labor relations, management reliability and performance, and its contribution to society, among other qualities.

Life-cycle stage variables

Life-cycle stage

Definition: The life-cycle stage of the industry in which the SBU competes. Life-cycle stage can be determined by its parameters or assessed directly.

In determining the life-cycle stage of an industry, as defined by the Hofer model (five stages), six variables may be used as parameters: market growth rate, rate of technological change in product, rate of technological change in process, change in market growth, market segmentation, and major functional concern. The following table provides values for the parameter variables that are indicative of each life-cycle stage.[7]

It is possible to assess the life-cycle stage directly, as one of the following:

- Development: not yet growing, or growing slightly,
- Growth: growing fast; exponential growth,
- Shakeout: growing fast but slowing down,
- Maturity: growth coming to a standstill,
- Decline: negative growth.

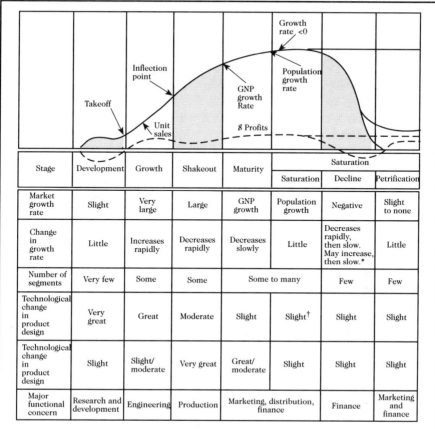

Stage	Development	Growth	Shakeout	Maturity	Saturation		
					Saturation	Decline	Petrification
Market growth rate	Slight	Very large	Large	GNP growth	Population growth	Negative	Slight to none
Change in growth rate	Little	Increases rapidly	Decreases rapidly	Decreases slowly	Little	Decreases rapidly, then slow. May increase, then slow.*	Little
Number of segments	Very few	Some	Some	Some to many		Few	Few
Technological change in product design	Very great	Great	Moderate	Slight	Slight†	Slight	Slight
Technological change in product design	Slight	Slight/ moderate	Very great	Great/ moderate	Slight	Slight	Slight
Major functional concern	Research and development	Engineering	Production	Marketing, distribution, finance		Finance	Marketing and finance

* The rate of change of the market growth rate usually only increases during the decline stage for those products that do not die, i.e., that enter the petrification stage of evolution.
† Although the rate of technological changes in the basic design of the product is usually low during this stage of market evolution, the probability of a major breakthrough to a different kind of product that performs the same function increase substantially during this period.

Figure 5.2   Product Life-Cycle Curve with Prescriptions for Functional Area Emphasis of Each Stage.

Reprinted from: C.W. Hofer, *Conceptual Constructs for Formulating Corporate and Business Strategy.* Boston: Intercollegiate Case Clearing House, 9-378-754, Boston, 1977, p. 7.

Change in market growth

Definition: Whether growth is declining (growing more slowly) or increasing (growing faster) or leveling off (neither increasing nor decreasing) is measured by the slope of the growth function.

Rate of technological change in product

Definition: The role and importance of the technology incorporated in the product's features and the rate at which it is changing are functions of the overall rate of technological change in the industry. In new industries the products are being changed frequently, since customers' needs are not yet known. In mature industries the rate of change in product technology has slowed down. Will a product become obsolete if it is not upgraded technologically? This depends on the life-cycle stage of the industry.

Rate of technological change in process

Definition: The role and importance of the technology utilized in the production process, and the rate at which it is changing. Whether or not an SBU will lose its competitive edge if it does not upgrade the technology of its production process depends on the life-cycle stage of the industry. During shakeout and maturity, upgrading of technological processes (rationalization) are a *must* for sustaining a competitive advantage. Most changes therefore occur during these stages.

Market segmentation

Definition: The degree to which the market is segmented. A highly segmented market, each segment serving customers with different needs, is very attractive, because it allows competitors to achieve advantages such as differential pricing, and to present many variations of the same product. It is attractive both to the large competitor, who may choose to target many segments, and to the small competitors wishing to target a niche.

Major functional concern – at present

Definition: The major area of planning and work, at the functional level, *of the industry in general* is based on the specific stage of the product–market evolution of the industry: research and development, engineering, production, marketing and distribution, finance.

Use of the model

The Hofer–Schendel model may be usefully applied to balancing the corporate portfolio and assigning business strategies to each SBU. Hofer and Schendel make a clear distinction between the corporate and business levels.

The model depicts an interactive top-down approach for analyzing multi-industry firms. The first step is to establish the desired corporate portfolio profile. The next step should be the formulation of specific business strategies for the separate SBUs. Afterwards, any gaps existing between corporate and SBU-level strategies are closed through consultation between managers at the two levels.

Another use of the model is competitor analysis at both corporate and business level. At the corporate level, Hofer and Schendel recommend full awareness of other corporations that might be searching for, or vulnerable

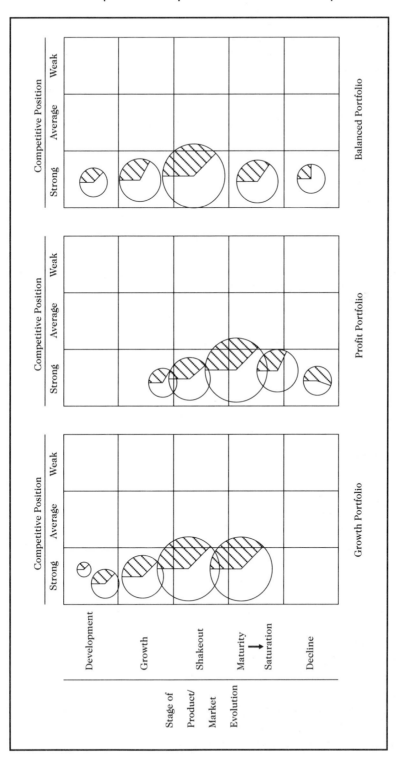

Figure 5.3 The three basic types of ideal corporate portfolios

to, a takeover. At the business level, they highly recommend that the competitors' possible reactions to specific strategies be taken into account.

Portfolio balancing

The basic issues of corporate strategies, according to Hofer and Schendel, address three types of sub-strategies: 1. corporate portfolio strategies; 2. resource procurement strategies; 3. corporate political strategies.

Corporate portfolio strategies are analogous to SBU strategies: how to meet the corporate goals, while allocating limited resources. As noted in the Planning Focus section, there are essentially three basic types of ideal portfolios: growth portfolios, profit portfolios, and balanced portfolios. These are graphically depicted in Figure 5.2.[8]

The term 'Winners' is borrowed from the GE/McKinsey model for strong (or average) SBUs in industries with high (or medium) attractiveness (it does not apply to average SBUs in medium industries). A 'Winner' according to the Hofer–Schendel matrix, as shown in the display of the three ideal portfolios, is a strong SBU with a relatively large market share (a large pie wedge).

Profit portfolios are characterized by low growth and high profit. They have many large established Winners with a few developing Winners. They usually have low debt/equity ratios and typically make high dividend payments.

Growth portfolios are characterized by high growth and moderate profit. They have just enough established Winners (high cash-flow producers) to support a large number of developing Winners. They usually have high debt/equity ratios and typically make low dividend payments.

Balanced portfolios are characterized by an even distribution of rising Winners in the development stage and established Winners in the maturity stage. In this case, the corporation is preparing for the future by investing in new Winners, while simultaneously using the established Winners to support the rising Winners. A pattern exists whereby the rising Winners of today will become the established Winners of tomorrow as the life cycle progresses.

The idea is to allocate resources according to the desired corporate strategy. Contrary to other portfolio models (particularly BCG), Hofer and Schendel assume that it is generally necessary to raise long-term external funding.

The resource-procurement strategy is based on four basic factors:

- The rate of internal fund generation,
- The rate of dividend payouts,
- The amount of new equity the corporation can raise,
- The corporate debt capacity.

Hofer and Schendel discuss actions that may be taken other than changing the portfolio strategy, such as changing the resource-procurement strategy, changing the political strategy, or changing the corporate objectives. For the present discussion we will assume that changing the portfolio strategy has been chosen as the course of action. Thus, the portfolio may be balanced by achieving one of the ideal portfolios in the following manner:

- Invest in newly evolving SBUs so that they can secure strong competitive positions in the future.

- Invest in average or weak SBUs in order to nurture them into strong competitive positions. Resource constraints will determine how many such SBUs the corporation can afford to cultivate.

- Harvest very weak SBUs in growth markets that are unlikely to attain strong positions in the future, weak SBUs in saturated or declining markets that are producing negative cash flows, and SBUs that are so different from the other SBUs in the corporation that top management cannot manage them effectively.

- Acquire new SBUs with strong competitive positions, if they do not exist internally. Acquisition decisions must take into consideration compatibility, synergies, and timing.

Concurrently with the above corporate strategies the corporation should:

- Maximize resource generation in accordance with the level of risk the main shareholders are willing to take.

- Develop political strategies to support the portfolio changes. In some cases, it may be necessary to change political strategies.

- Change the corporate objectives. This of course is only used as a last resort, when all other alternatives have failed.

Hofer and Schendel[9] identify four archetypical unbalanced portfolios and their characteristics:

1. A portfolio with too many weak SBUs in later stages of the life cycle often suffers from insufficient cash flow, profits and growth.

2. An excess of weak SBUs in early stages of the life cycle leads to deficient cash flow and profits.

3. Too many strong, established SBUs produce surplus cash flow but provide no growth areas for investment.

4. A portfolio with a profusion of developing, potentially strong SBUs demands a great amount of attention and offers negative cash flow and unstable growth and profits in return.

In general, unbalanced portfolios produce less stable, less reliable growth and profits and involve greater corporate risk than balanced portfolios.

SBU strategic planning

At the business level the Hofer–Schendel matrix is used for SBU strategic planning with the six generic strategies described above, according to the SBU's position within the matrix.

Table 5.1 summarizes the characteristics of the strategies.[10]

Table 5.1

Characteristics of the Six Generic Business Strategies

Type of Generic Strategy	Competitive Position Objective	Investment Strategy
Share-increasing strategies		
Development stage	Increase position	Moderate investment
Shake-out stage	Increase position	High investment
Other stages	Increase position	Very high investment
Growth strategies	Maintain position	High investment
Profit strategies	Maintain position	Moderate investment
Market concentration and asset reduction strategies	Reduce (shift) position to smaller defensible level (niche)	Moderate to negative investment*
Liquidation or divestiture strategies	Decrease position to zero	Negative investment
Turnaround strategies	Improve positions	Little to moderate investment*

* Usually, some new assets are required, while others are sold off. The net level of investment depends upon the relative proportion of these two activities in each specific case.

Model's assumptions, limitations and misuse, and critique

Assumptions

The basic assumption of the business-level analysis is that a typical industry life cycle exists, or, as Hofer and Schendel call it, the product–market evolution curve. The life-cycle curve follows the S-shaped sales curve. The points of inflection on the sales curve indicate the beginning of stages that provide the best opportunities for rapid expansion, namely development, shakeout and decline.[11, 12]

Hofer and Schendel assume that the SBUs are related to one another, and that their life cycles are therefore somewhat similar. If, however, the SBUs are not closely related, Hofer and Schendel[13] recommend switching over to the GE/McKinsey matrix for corporate-level analysis and strategy formulation.

One of the basic assumptions of the Hofer–Schendel model is that the corporation cannot, generally speaking, raise internal funding for long-term investment strategies, and must seek external funding. Thus, the cash balance of the corporation does not have to reside on zero. The following principles are used as assumptions by Hofer and Schendel:

- Budgeting and implementation planning are excluded from the strategy-formulation process.

- Social and political inputs must be included in the strategy-formulation process. At the business level they recommend including these inputs after economic, demographic and technological analyses have been performed. Technological innovation, for example, may push a mature product/SBU back into another period of rapid growth.[14]

- Contingency plans must be devised at both the business and corporate levels, taking into account environmental turbulence and uncertainty. As we will see, this last point contradicts the ADL approach, in which the authors try to create a linkage between the conception and the pursuit of strategies. The Hofer–Schendel approach is considered academic, rather than empirical, on this matter.

Limitations and misuse

The market growth rate must be measured in deflated dollars and not in current dollars, otherwise the real picture of growth is distorted, and the product evolution stage may be misjudged. As the table of six variables is the main tool for assessing the product stage, it is extremely important not to distort these figures.

Hofer and Schendel themselves are the first to note that their matrix cannot be used on its own. They highly recommend using the GE/McKinsey model for analysis at the corporate level for corporations with SBUs that are not related to one another, as market attractiveness provides a broader base for comparing completely different industries than does the product–market evolution stage. Another situation in which they recommend using the GE/McKinsey model is when turnaround strategies are being contemplated: here the GE/McKinsey model is used for assessing industry attractiveness.

Hofer and Schendel warn against using their model for predicting winning strategies.[15] They note the subtle difference between determining what strategy should be adopted and predicting if it can succeed, stressing that they have only described the common characteristics of the remaining (successful) rivals.

Critique: Benefits and drawbacks

One of the benefits of the Hofer–Schendel matrix, as noted by Chang and Campo-Flores,[16] is that it incorporates the two relevant dimensions of the BCG and GE models – competitive position and market attractiveness (the size of the circles), and adds a third dimension – the product–market evolution. Glueck and Jauch[17] agree that the single most important variable influencing the strategy to be taken is the stage of the product–market life cycle. The life-cycle curve is quite consistent in most industries, the main variations being in the length of the stages, and the level of sales/profits generated at each stage.[18, 19]

Very few empirical studies have been carried out to validate the Hofer–Schendel matrix. As already noted, it relies heavily on the GE/McKinsey model, using industry attractiveness as an important factor. Although the Hofer–Schendel model apparently cannot stand alone, its contribution to the analysis of the life-cycle concept is substantial, both in terms of the refined division of the stages and in the explicit, clear-cut table the authors have developed for assessing the product–market evolution stage.

As we have seen, the generic strategies spread over more than one cell of the matrix. The differences between a strong, an average and a weak SBU adopting a certain generic strategy are not addressed. In general the authors seem to be suggesting 'what to do' but not 'how to do it'. In their table of recommended investment strategies they make no distinction whatsoever between the recommendations for strong and average SBUs at any specific life-cycle stage. The table could be reduced to two categories – strong and weak – with no loss of information.

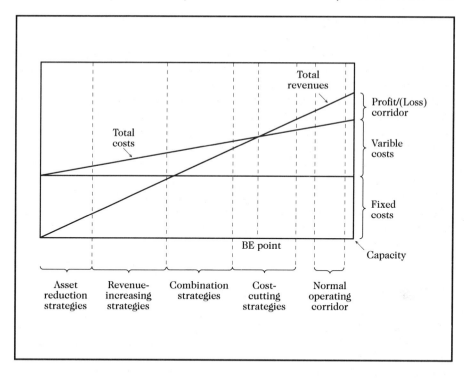

Figure 5.4 Strategic alternatives for closing business strategic gaps

Reprinted by permission from: C.W. Hofer, 'Turnaround Strategies' *The Journal Of Business Strategy*, Vol 1, no. 1 Copyright © 1980 by Warren, Gorham and Lamont, Inc., 210 South St., Boston, Mass. All rights reserved.

Variations and additions

Additional variables

Industry analysis at the business level is an important issue in the Hofer–Schendel approach, and should therefore be carried out in addition to the assessment of the product–market evolution stage.

Their industry analysis would measure the following variables:

- Product differentiation
- Characteristics of competition
- Customer value

- Technological barriers to entry
- Entrance barriers – non-technological
- Technology development

In addition, their industry analysis includes a variable that measures the level of capital intensity of the industry.[20]

Additions

Hofer has added a break-even diagram (fixed costs, variable costs, revenues, and so on) for determining which strategic alternative should be implemented in order to 'close gaps' and turn the business around. The diagram in Figure 5.3 displays recommendations as to when asset reduction, revenue increasing, combination, and cost-cutting strategies should be adopted. Businesses operating well below the break-even point will be forced to apply more drastic measures.[21, 22]

6

The ADL Life-Cycle model

History: Development and use

The ADL Life-Cycle Model was developed by Arthur D. Little, Inc., a well-known management consulting group based in Cambridge, Mass. This structured methodology for analyzing current strategy and for strategic planning is a powerful portfolio analysis tool for a diversified multi-unit corporation, and is used and implemented at both the corporate and the business-unit level.[1]

According to ADL's life-cycle concept, an industry typically goes through the following four chronological stages: embryonic, growth, maturity and aging. The basic assumption of the model is that an SBU (termed a strategic center by ADL) may be at any one of the different stages of the product life cycle, and must therefore be analyzed accordingly.[2]

In addition to these changes in the life cycle of the industry, the competitive position of the SBU may change, relative to the other SBUs competing in the same industry. The SBU is classified as holding one of five basic competitive positions: dominant, strong, favorable, tenable, or weak. A sixth position – nonviable – is not handled in detail by ADL and is dropped altogether here.

Each SBU is analyzed separately to determine the development stage of its industry, and its competitive position within this industry. The combination of these two multifactor dimensions – the four industry life-cycle stages and the five competitive positions – constitutes the Arthur D. Little 20-cell matrix.[3]

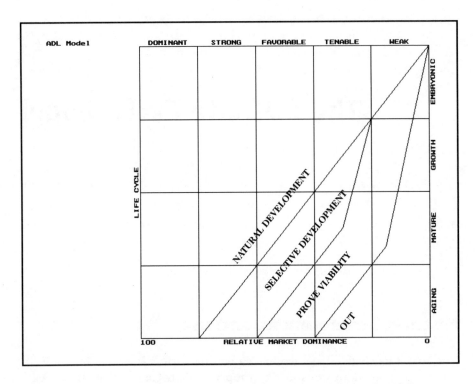

Figure 6.1   ADL model (Arthur D. Little, Inc. Permission August 12, 1994).

The specific positioning of each SBU is displayed on a single grid, along with all the other corporate SBUs. ADL proposes a very elaborate set of strategic planning options for the business level, based on the position of the SBU in the matrix.

The planning of strategies is performed in three consecutive steps. First, the 'natural thrust' of the SBU is determined solely by its position on the ADL matrix. A natural thrust covers a number of cells. Second, within each natural thrust, the position of the cell determines a 'specific thrust'. A specific thrust is still a very general strategic guideline, such as 'invest selectively for growth'. The third step, which is ADL's unique contribution to portfolio planning, is to choose a generic strategy. This is a 'step down' from strategic planning to operational planning. ADL offers a menu of so-called generic strategies, suitable for each specific thrust. The generic strategies are stated in operational terms such as 'develop an overseas business'. ADL names 24 such strategies.

The planning focus: RONA

The basic concept of the ADL model is that the corporate's portfolio – as depicted by life-cycle stage and competitive position – should be balanced. A balanced portfolio according to the ADL model has the following attributes:

1. Its SBUs are distributed throughout all stages of the life cycle.

2. The cash flow is positive: there is at least as much cash generation (from mature and aging SBUs) as there is cash usage (from embryonic and growth SBUs).

3. The average weighted return on net assets (RONA) of all SBUs meets corporate goals.

4. The more dominant, strong and favorable SBUs there are, the better the portfolio.

A portfolio that consists of only mature and aging SBUs with viable competitive positions is probably producing positive cash flows and high profits at present, but promises little for the future. A portfolio comprising only embryonic and growing SBUs has a promising future, but may have a negative cash flow at present.

ADL uses an auxiliary graph called a 'Ronagraph' for balancing the portfolio. This two-dimensional graph is comprised of RONA in percentages and internal deployment of funds (reinvestment). Its application is discussed later in the Use section of this chapter. The concept of analyzing RONA vs. cash flow is unique to ADL, and it is one of the model's contributions to portfolio analysis.

Use and display of the matrix

Dimensions

For compatibility with the other models in this book, the ADL matrix is composed of industry maturity on the Y axis and competitive positioning of the SBU on the X axis.

Y Axis: Industry maturity

Industry maturity is defined as the impact of certain external forces on the business, as summarized by the four stages of the business life cycle.

These forces are generally not within the control of the SBU, though it may influence them under certain conditions, for example, by repositioning a product in its mature stage, or introducing a new product, based on new technologies.

The various stages of the life cycle of an industry are characterized by the development over time (that is, rates of change) in sales, cash flows, and profits of the industry as a whole.[4]

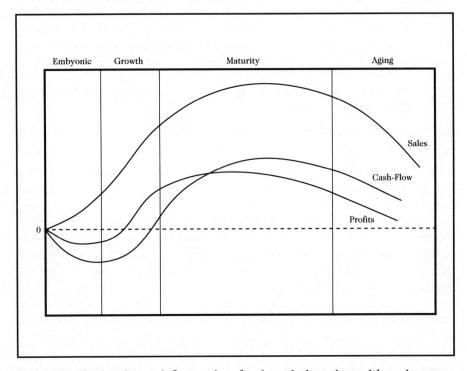

Figure 6.2 Yearly sales, cash flow, and profits through the industry life-cycle stages.

Reprinted from: Hax, Arnoldo C. and Majluf, Nicolas S. (1984). *Strategic Management: An Integrative Perspective.* Englewood Cliffs, NJ: Prentice-Hall, p. 183. (Arthur D. Little, Inc. Permission August 12, 1994).

The four stages of industry maturity can be described as follows:

Embryonic

An embryonic industry is one that has recently been established, in recognition of an unfulfilled need of a group of customers, or by developing product–markets based on new technologies that previously did not exist, or were not utilized, to fulfil certain customer needs. The main characteristics of such an industry are 'changes in technology, great pursuit of new customers, and fragmented and changing shares of market.'[5] Sales are increasing rapidly, profits are negative, and cash flows are even more negative.

Growth

In the growth stage, the products of the industry are being accepted by ever-growing numbers of customers, and competitors are fighting hard to gain larger shares of the 'expanding pie'. At the growth stage 'customers, shares and technology are better known and entry into the industry is more difficult.'[5] Sales are increasing very rapidly, profits have become positive and are growing rapidly, though cash flows may still be negative.

Maturity

Maturity represents a stage of saturation of the market. All or most of the potential customers are already purchasing the product, and at relatively regular intervals. Maturity is characterized by 'stability in known customers, technology and shares of market, although the industry may still be market competitive.'[5] Sales reach a peak via slower growth and then level off, profits reach a peak and level off or start a slow decline, while cash flows become and remain positive.

Aging

An aging market is one in which the customers are losing interest in the products, either because new and better substitutes are fulfiling the same needs, or perhaps because of a change in consumer needs or tastes. The main characteristics are 'falling demand, a declining number of competitors, and in many such industries, a narrowing of the product line.'[5] Sales are dropping drastically, profits are dropping, and cash flows are dropping slowly; all are converging towards zero.

X Axis: Competitive positioning of the SBU in the industry

Competitive position is defined broadly as the strength, from dominant to weak, of an SBU relative to other SBUs competing in the same market. This strength is revealed by the degree of freedom the SBU has in choosing its strategy, as well as the degree of control it has over the strategies of other SBUs.

The five categories of competitive position (and the sixth one, which has been dropped here) may be described as follows:

Dominant

Only one SBU, if any, can hold this position in a given industry. The position often results from a quasi-monopoly or a strongly protected technological leadership. This type of SBU (if it exists) sets the standard for the industry and controls the behavior of other competitors. A dominant SBU has the choice of a wide range of strategic options.[6]

Strong

A strong SBU is one that can usually follow strategies of its own choice, irrespective of the moves of its competitors, and enjoys a definite advantage over its competitors. Relative market share is at least 1.5 times that of its largest direct competitor, but it does not have absolute dominance.

Favorable

This is an SBU with something unique about its business. It is among the leaders in a less concentrated industry, where no competitor clearly stands out or dominates. When in a niche, this type of SBU is relatively safe from attack, and is usually capable of improving its competitive situation.

Tenable

This is an SBU that maintains a profitable position by specializing in a narrow and reasonably protected niche, be it a market segment specialization or a product specialization. A tenable SBU maintains its position, but is unlikely to improve it.

Weak

This is an SBU that suffers from a critical weakness that prevents it from becoming profitable in the long run. The weakness may be intrinsic (the SBU may be too small or lack important resources) or it may be due to past mistakes. In either case the SBU cannot survive independently, given the competitive economics of the industry.

Nonviable

This is an SBU that has no present or future strength whatsoever. The only strategic response possible for such an SBU, apart from divestment, is to prolong its existence. Since the options are so clear, this book does not deal with this competitive position.

Description of the ADL matrix cells

The ADL is thus a 5×4 grid on which all the SBUs of the corporation are placed according to their industry life-cycle stages and competitive positions.

The matrix display has several functions. In addition to presenting the overall corporate mix of SBUs, several direct implications pertain to each cell in the matrix:

1.   Each cell is associated with typical profitability and cash flow.

2.   Each cell implies strategic guidelines for market share, strategic positioning[7] and required investments.

3. Each cell falls into a 'natural thrust' domain, which in turn determines the possible 'specific thrusts' and a number of 'generic strategies' that may be implemented by the SBU. In cells that cover two (or more) natural thrusts (*see* diagonal borders in Figure 6.1), two (or more) specific thrusts are relevant for the cell. In these cases, we describe all strategic guidelines.

Each cell encompasses:

- Typical profitability and cash flow,

- The natural thrusts to which the cell belongs,

- Strategic guidelines matched with specific thrusts (codes – from A to X – of suitable generic strategies, detailed in the following table),

- Typical investment requirements for pursuing these guidelines.

Generic Strategies proposed by Arthur D. Little, Inc.

Survey Code

A	Backward Integration
B	Development of Overseas Business
C	Development of Overseas Facilities
D	Distribution Rationalization
E	Excess Capacity
F	Export/Same Product
G	Forward Integration
H	Hesitation
I	Initial Market Development
J	Licensing Abroad
K	Complete Rationalization
L	Market Penetration
M	Market Rationalization
N	Methods and Functions Efficiency
O	New Products/New Markets
P	New Products/Same Markets
Q	Production Rationalization
R	Product Line Rationalization
S	Pure Survival
T	Same products/New Markets
U	Same Products/Same Markets
V	Technological Efficiency
W	Traditional Cost Cutting Efficiency
X	Unit Abandonment

Following is a description of the 20 cells in the ADL matrix. All cells that are divided diagonally across will have two (or more) natural thrusts. Thus, **Strong/Aging**, for example, is divided between natural development and selective development. The manager, after more detailed analysis, may pursue either option, as best suits the specific SBU, since these are border-line cases.

Dominant/Embryonic
Probably, but not necessarily, profitable. Net cash borrower.
Natural development may be pursued by:
All-out push for share – Fast Growth (B, C, E, G, L, N, O, P, T, V) or
Hold position - Start Up (E, I, L).
Invest slightly faster than the market dictates.

Dominant/Growth
Profitable. Probably, but not necessarily, net cash producer.
Natural development may be pursued by:
Hold position – Attain Cost Leadership (A, C, N, U, V, W), or
Hold share – Defend Position (A, C, N, U, V, W).
Invest to sustain growth rate (and preempt new competitors and possible entrants.

Profitable
Probably, but not necessarily, net cash producer.
Natural development may be pursued by:
Hold position – Attain Cost Leadership (A, C, N, U, V, W), or
Hold share – Defend Position (A, C, N, U, V, W).
Invest to sustain growth rate (and preempt new competitors and possible entrants).

Dominant/Mature
Profitable. Net cash producer.
Natural development may be pursued by:
Hold share – Grow With Industry (A, B, C, F, G, J, N, P, T, U), or
Hold position – Defend Position (A, C, N, U, V, W).
Reinvest as necessary.

Dominant/Aging
Profitable. Net cash producer.
Natural development may be pursued by:
Hold position – Defend Position (A, C, N, U, V, W).
Reinvest as necessary

Strong/Embryonic
May be unprofitable. Net cash borrower.
Natural development may be pursued by:
Attempt to improve position – Start Up (E, I, L) or,

All-out push for share – Fast Growth (B, C, E, G, L, N, O, P, T, V).
Invest as fast as the market dictates.

Strong/Growth
Probably profitable. Probably net cash borrower.
Natural development may be pursued by:
Attempt to improve position – Attain Cost Leadership (A, C, N, U, V, W), or
Push for share – Fast Growth (B, C, E, G, L, N, O, P, T, V).
Invest to increase growth rate (and improve position).

Strong/Mature
Profitable. Net cash producer.
Natural development (selective development) may be pursued by:
Hold position – Defend Position (A, C, N, U, V, W), or
Hold share – Grow With Industry (A, B, C, F, G, J, N, P, T, U).
Reinvest as necessary.

Strong/Aging
Profitable. Net cash producer.
Natural development may be pursued by:
Hold position – Defend Position (A, C, N, U, V, W), or
Harvest (D, H, K, M, Q, R, V, W).
Selective development may be pursued by:
Hang In – Hold On To Niche (C, D, N, Q, U).
Minimum reinvestment or maintenance.

Favorable/Embryonic
Probably unprofitable. Net cash borrower.
Natural development may be pursued by:
Selective push for share – Focus, gain position gradually, or
All out push for share - Fast Growth (B, C, E, G, L, N, O, P, T, V).
Invest selectively.

Favorable/Growth
Marginally profitable. Net cash borrower.
Natural development may be pursued by:
Attempt to improve position – Cost Leadership In Focus Market (A, C, N, U, V, W).
Selective development may be pursued by:
Selective push for share – (gradually) Differentiate, Focus.
Selective investment to improve position.

Favorable/Mature
Moderately profitable. Net cash producer.
Natural development may be pursued by:
Custodial or Maintenance – Grow With Industry (A, B, C, F, G, J, N, P, T, U).

Selective development may be pursued by:
Find Niche and Protect It (A, G, I, L, M, R, T), or
Prove Viability.
Minimum and/or selective reinvestment.

Favorable/Aging
Moderately profitable. Cash flow balanced.
Selective development may be pursued by:
Harvest – Exploit Niche (B, C, E, L, N, P, U, V), or
Hang In – Hold Niche (C, D, N, Q, U), or
Phased withdrawal – Withdraw (D, M, Q, R, W).
Minimum maintenance investment or divest.

Tenable/Embryonic
Unprofitable. Net cash borrower.
Natural development or selective development may be pursued by:
Selectively pushing for position – Focus (G, L, T), or
Prove Viability.
Invest very selectively.

Tenable/Growth
Unprofitable. Net cash borrower or cash flow balanced.
Natural development or selective development may be pursued by:
Selectively pushing for position – Focus, Differentiate (G, L, T), or
Find Niche and Protect It (A, G, I, L, M, R, T), or
Prove Viability by:
Aggressively pushing for share – Catch up (D, E, L, M, P, Q, R).
Selective investment.

Tenable/Mature
Minimally profitable. Cash flow balanced.
Selective development may be pursued by:
Find niche and hang on – Hold Niche (C, D, N, Q, U)
If viability is not proven the recommendation is Out by:
Phased withdrawal – Withdraw (D, M, Q, R, W).
Minimum reinvestment or divest.

Tenable/Aging
Minimally profitable. Cash flow balanced.
If viability is not proven the recommendation is Out by:
Phased withdrawal – Withdraw (D, M, Q, R, W), or
Abandon – Abandon (X).
Disinvest or divest.

Weak/Embryonic
Unprofitable. Net cash borrower.
Viability may be proven by:

Up – Catch up (D, E, L, M, P, Q, R). If not, then:
Out – Withdraw (D, M, Q, R, W), or
Out – Divest (D, K, Q, R, S).
Invest or divest.

Weak/Growth

Unprofitable. Net cash borrower or cash flow balanced.
Prove viability by:
Turnaround (D, L, M, N, Q, R, V, W), or
Renew (D, M, O, P, Q, R, U).
If viability cannot be proven then Out by:
Abandon (X).
Invest or divest.

Weak/Mature

Unprofitable. May be net cash borrower or net cash producer.
Prove viability:
Turnaround (D, L, M, N, Q, R, V, W), or
Renew (D, M, O, P, Q, R, U).
If viability cannot be proven then Out:
Phased withdrawal – Withdraw (D, M, Q, R, W).
Invest selectively or, divest.

Weak/Aging

Unprofitable (writeoff).
Out: Abandon (X).
Divest.

Relevant strategic variables

To use the ADL Life-Cycle Model, values for the following variables should
be assigned.

Business strength variables (X axis)	Life-cycle stage variables (Y axis)
Overall competitive position	Life-cycle stage
Patents	Market growth rate
Production efficiency	Characteristics of competition
After-sales service	Customer brand loyalty
Vertical integration	Market share stability
Management's attitude to risk	Entrance barriers – non-technological
	Product line breadth
	Technology development

The following are the definitions and measurements of the new variables not defined in the previous chapters.

Business strength variables

Overall competitive position

The overall competitive position for the ADL model (competitive positions were listed and described earlier in this chapter) is determined, as for all other portfolio matrix models, as a weighted average of the business strength variables included in the model. However, in the ADL model the overall competitive position can be assessed directly as: nonviable, weak, tenable, favorable, strong, dominant.

Management's attitude to risk

Definition: In its decision making on issues such as entering new markets, introduction of new products, and so on, management may be a risk taker or risk averse.

Life-cycle stage variables

Life-cycle stage ADL

Definition: The life cycle stage of the industry in which the SBU competes. Life-cycle stage can be determined by its parameters or assessed directly.

In determining the life-cycle stage of an industry, as defined by the ADL model (four stages), seven variables may be used as parameters: market growth rate, characteristics of competition, customer brand loyalty, market share stability, entrance barriers, product line breadth and technology development. The following table provides values for the variables that are indicative of each life-cycle stage.[8, 9, 10] It is possible to assess the life-cycle stage directly as one of the following:

Embryonic: not yet growing, or growing slightly

Growth: growing fast; exponential growth

Maturity: growth coming to a standstill

Aging: negative growth

Market share stability

Definition: The number and frequency of new entrants or exits of present competitors. It is the distribution of market share among competitors, and the stability of this distribution.

Values for the variables that are indicative of each life-cycle stage

Stage of Maturity / Factor	Embryonic	Growth	Mature	Ageing
Growth Rate	?	> GNP	≤ GNP	< 0
Predictability of Growth	?	Uncertain	Well Known	Well Known
Product Line	Basic	Proliferating	Being Renewed	Shrinking
Competitors	Increasing	Large Number and Increasing, Then Decreasing	Few and Stable	Declining
Market Shares	Fragmented	Fragmented; Some Leaders	Concentration	More Concentration
Stability of Market Share	Volatile	Leaders Switching Position	Leaders Entrenched	High Stability
Customer Stability	Little or None	Some; Buyers Aggressive	High Loyalty-Buying Pattern Established	Stable
Ease of Entry	Very Easy	Usually Easy	Difficult	Difficult Unattractive
Technology	Concept Development, Product Engineering	Product Line Refinement and Extension	Product Line Renewal; Processes and Materials	Minimal

Reprinted from: *Long Range Planning*, 17, Younger, M. 'Assessing opportunities for diversification – an analytical approach', p. 13, © Copyright 1984, with kind permission from Elsevier Science Ltd.

Entrance barriers – other than technological (branding, distribution, financial, political, legal, …)

Definition: The ease with which a new competitor can enter the market is measured by the number and intensity of entrance barriers, which may be legal requirements, meeting high regulatory/technological standards, high capital requirements, fierce bargaining power of existing competitors, expenses involved in creating a brand name and establishing distribution channels. In general, high entrance barriers are associated with high industry profitability. The viewpoint is that of an existing manufacturer.

Product line breadth

Definition: The relative number and diversity of products in the *industry*, and the extent to which it is expanding or contracting.

Technology development

Definition: The degree to which the industry has stabilized on one or more major product or process technologies. At the lower end of the scale is an industry characterized by many, frequently switched technologies.

Use of the model

The ADL model is used to display the status of each SBU in terms of its competitive position and the life-cycle stage of its product markets, to balance the corporate portfolio for resource allocation strategies, and to match specific strategies to each SBU at the business level.

Balancing the Life-Cycle Matrix

In addition to the presentation of the competitive position and life-cycle stage of the SBU, ADL uses the matrix format in order to exhibit the financial contribution of each cell of the grid to the corporate portfolio. The matrix is used to display the distribution of sales, net income, assets and RONA by life-cycle stage and competitive positioning. The figure in the cell represents the contribution of that cell to the specific financial indicator; sales and assets are given as a percent of total corporate sales and assets. For example, the relative contribution of a cell to corporate sales would be calculated as follows:

$$\frac{\Sigma \text{ sales of SBUs in cell } (\$) \times 100}{\Sigma \text{ sales of SBUs in portfolio } (\$)}$$

The subtotals for the different competitive position columns (for dominant SBUs, strong SBUs, and so on) and subtotals for the different life-cycle stage rows (for embryonic SBUs, growth SBUs, and so on) are displayed in the margins.

A balanced portfolio is judged by the relative distribution of financial indicators along the life-cycle dimension (the subtotal for each row). If, for example, the SBUs in the aging stage account for 70% of corporate sales, the portfolio is very unbalanced.

Balancing the Ronagraph

The Ronagraph is a graphical display of the performance of the SBUs – in terms of their RONA – and the level of reinvestment of cash (internal redeployment) into the SBU or contribution of cash to other SBUs in the corporation.

Internal deployment is the relative percentage of funds reinvested in the SBU. It is the change in assets divided by the operating funds flow, presented as a percentage, where the change in assets is the assets (including depreciation) of the current year minus those of the previous year, and the operating funds flow is profit after taxes with depreciation added back on.

There are four typical types of cash redeployment: cash generators, cash users, cash neutral units, and units with negative internal deployment (that is, a divestment strategy is being applied: operating cash flow is positive, while assets are reduced):

1. Cash generator – internal deployment significantly less than 100.
2. Cash user – internal deployment significantly greater than 100.
3. Cash neutral – internal deployment of around 100.
4. Negative internal deployment – reinvestment (numerator) is negative.

The Ronagraph is used to balance the portfolio by validating that SBUs appear in the expected positions for each stage of the life cycle. For example, embryonic SBUs have a very low or negative RONA, and are very high cash users. Similarly, SBUs at other stages have different and characteristic RONAs and internal deployment figures.

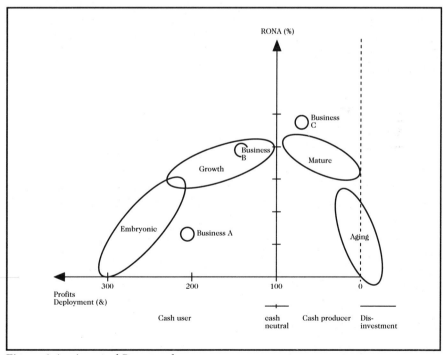

Figure 6.4 A typical Ronagraph.

Reprinted from: Hax, Arnoldo C. and Majluf, Nicolas S. (1984). *Strategic Management: An Integrative Perspective.* Englewood Cliffs, NJ: Prentice-Hall, p. 201. (Arthur D. Little, Inc. Permission August 12, 1994).

A balanced portfolio should have SBUs in all four typical groupings. An acceptable Ronagraph depicts a balanced portfolio and adequate profitability, that is:

1.   Cash flow generation is greater than or equal to cash flow usage.

2.   The average weighted RONA is commensurate with corporate goals.[11]

The portfolio balance may be judged by visually examining the Ronagraph to ascertain the existence of SBUs in the appropriate positions.

SBU strategic planning

The Ronagraph may also be usefully applied at the business level. SBUs should fall into groups on the Ronagraph, each group representing a stage in the industry life cycle with its usual implications for cash flows and return on investment. If an SBU falls far from the expected curve, it should be given special attention.

For example, an SBU that is a cash user, even though it has been identified as belonging to a mature industry, is behaving peculiarly. The reasons for such performance should be examined, and appropriate action taken.

The working concept is that each SBU requires its own strategic planning and positioning, and is therefore analyzed separately. Each SBU receives its own strategic recommendations, which are derived manually from the ADL planning model in the following three consecutive steps:

1.   Check the natural thrust to which each SBU belongs.

2.   Determine the specific thrust suitable to managerial objectives, investment requirements and expected results.

3.   Choose an operational strategy from the list of generic strategies, suitable to the natural thrust and the specific thrust.

At the business level each SBU should choose a strategy based on its positioning in the ADL matrix and its business objectives. A specific strategy for an SBU is a function of the following business objectives:

• Desired market share,

• Financial resources to support investments,

• Expected profitability and cash flows required from or contributed to the corporation.

Assumptions

The ADL approach assumes that most industries follow the life-cycle pattern in the prescribed order, though the length of the cycle may vary from one industry to another. In some traditional industries the maturity stage can last for decades, and in some high-tech industries the whole cycle may be completed within a few years or even months. Experience has shown that products in the embryonic and growth stages are typically cash users and products in the maturity and aging stages are typically cash generators. It is also fair to say that younger and weaker SBUs are subject to higher risk levels than more mature and stronger SBUs.

According to the ADL model, mature industries comprise a small number of concentrated competitors, whereas embryonic industries are fragmented, with many competitors. This assumption will be challenged in the critique section.

Two basic assumptions regarding the corporation are that available resources are allocated among its various SBUs, and that the businesses within the corporation do not compete with one another.

Critique: Benefits and drawbacks

Benefits of the ADL model

The benefits of following all of ADL's analytical stages are: 1. proper definition of the function, market, position, and contribution of each SBU as part of the total, in a systematic and standardized method; (2) display of a complete picture of the portfolio, without losing sight of the specific strategies designated for each SBU. The ADL model's main benefit is also its main drawback: its approach is very systematic and can be accepted by the uninitiated as a strategic planning panacea. The general intention of the model is to provide the business manager with a menu of reasonable strategic alternatives for a complex matrix of SBUs.

Since it uses a life-cycle approach from start to end, the ADL model may be universally applied to different types of businesses. If the analysis places an SBU at a certain stage in the life cycle, then the recommendations will be suitable for that particular stage. One of the most common pitfalls of other portfolio models is that by ignoring the life-cycle stage they produce an 'average' analysis for all SBUs, whether they are in new markets or aging markets. ADL's contribution has been to raise the widely accepted life-cycle concept to a prominent position in strategic planning, thus allowing for specific strategic planning and not 'averaged out' strategic planning for SBUs at different stages.

A previously accepted common belief was that all units bringing a certain level of ROI, say 15%, were fulfiling corporate goals. The ADL approach demonstrates that this goal is inappropriate for some stages of the life cycle, for certain product markets, and is not compatible with many of the generic strategies listed by ADL. The ADL approach is particularly useful for high-tech industries in which the life cycles are very short, and for which, if the proper strategies are not taken at the proper time, the SBU could fall short of its goals.

Drawbacks of the ADL model

As the model is based on the length and stage of the life cycle, which vary from industry to industry and are difficult to ascertain, it can lead to inaccurate conclusions.

Limitations and misuse

The life cycle of a single product, and certainly of a whole industry, do not always follow the typical S-shaped function, as depicted in Figure 6.2. Prevailing economic conditions can blur the actual state of the industry, rendering our assessment of the industry life-cycle stage invalid. Basing strategic planning mainly on the life-cycle stage can thus lead to bias. Some authors have questioned the usefulness of the life-cycle approach, on the grounds that it tends to push managers to abandon existing products when sales decline, on the erroneous assumption that the aging stage has set in. Of course this assumption is not always correct, and the real reason for declining sales must be ascertained. For example, there could be a difference between brand sales behavior and total SBU sales as well as between the SBU pattern and the industry curve, leading to incorrect conclusions.

The assumption that firms do not influence the life-cycle stage can lead a manager to ignore certain strategies. In practice, firms can affect the life cycle. For example, the life-cycle course can be diverted by repositioning mature products or by adding innovations. The ADL model therefore seems to be limited only to strategies that do not endeavor to change the life cycle. For instance, mature markets can turn into growth markets (new uses for the bicycle). Mechanistic adherence to ADL does not allow for this possibility.

The structure of the competition (fragmented or concentrated) as a function of the life-cycle stage can vary from industry to industry. Some industries, particularly capital-intensive ones such as the automobile industry, begin as highly fragmented in the embryonic stage and become concentrated in maturity. Other industries, such as bank cash dispensers, have started out concentrated and become more fragmented later on. This contradicts the basic assumption of the ADL approach, according to which competition is fragmented during the embryonic stage (*see* Table p.109). The market being assessed must be carefully investigated, and a variable may be dropped if it does not comply with the ADL definition.[12]

As noted above, the main drawback of the ADL model is that it is very structured and could lead inexperienced managers to mechanistic and uncreative solutions. The large number of cells in the ADL matrix (20), and the three stages of analysis for planning, combined with the fact that a corporation has many SBUs, could make strategic planning a very tedious project for even the most experienced manager. An experienced manager will probably use the strategic guidelines as stimuli to develop several different strategic options. Inexperienced managers might be so baffled by the complexity of the model that they resort to following the instructions as a step-by-step action blueprint, thus losing the possibility of developing different, more creative solutions.

As already noted, the list of 24 generic strategies is not exhaustive.

ADL uses an abundance of different terms. For example: the specific strategy Prolong Existence is suitable for a strategic thrust called 'Hang In', which does not appear in either of the strategic thrust tables. We assume that this strategy is appropriate for mature SBUs that are relatively weak, as well as for aging SBUs that are rather strong. As another example, the term 'Harvest' is used for the Aging/Favorable cell.[13, 14] However, this cell falls into the Selective Development family, while Harvest is also a specific strategy belonging to the Natural Development family. We have chosen to interpret the former as 'harvest in a niche', possibly compatible with 'Exploit Niche'.

Another criticism of the ADL model relates to the seemingly arbitrary fashion in which the diagonals, which determine the natural strategic thrust of a cell, are drawn across the matrix. ADL provides no account of the considerations underlying the decision of where to draw these lines. Certain cells in the matrix are cut across by two diagonals, placing the cell within three natural strategic thrusts.

Variations and additions

Several authors have added measures for assessing competitive position. Younger[15] addresses four groups of variables, which may be used to assess the competitive position of the SBU. The executive should operationalize these variables according to the specific industry. The four groups are:

- **Brand**
  All competitive strengths associated with the SBU's brand names, including reputation in the eyes of the consumer.

- **Marketing/promotion**
  All marketing strengths such as skills in advertising, promotion, product development and packaging design.

- **Distribution power**
  All strengths relating to the company's existing distribution links with retail and wholesale channels, such as its reputation with the trade, its sales force, its retail skills and its physical distribution network.

- **Technical**
  All technical strengths in product technology, production, processing, and purchasing of raw materials. Osell and Wright speak of the following five main measures for assessing the competitive position: share of the market, technology, breadth of product line, market-share movement, and special market relations.

Younger[15] has a variation on the market-share variable for defining the life-cycle stage of the industry. He divides it into two separate variables: Market Share and Market Share Stability. It should be noted that Younger developed this later version of the ADL model in the course of his work as a consultant at ADL.

7

Incorporating risk into the portfolio matrix

Introduction

The next two chapters concentrate on the incorporation of risk into the evaluation of business portfolio strategies. This chapter reviews the treatment of risk in the portfolio models discussed in previous chapters: BCG, GE/McKinsey, Hofer–Schendel and ADL. Following this discussion, the chapter introduces the Risk Matrix developed by Hussey. Hussey based his model on the Directional Policy Matrix, to which he added risk as a third dimension. By virtue of its unique contribution, we have chosen to incorporate the Risk Matrix as a separate model in this book.

We will first discuss the importance of risk, detailing the various definitions of the term and how it is dealt with by the previous portfolio matrices.

Why risk?

One of the underlying concepts of the portfolio approach is that risk may be spread over a prospective strategy, to ensure a certain stability of sales and profits. Risk spreading may take any one of a number of forms:

- Diversification – to avoid dependence on a single line/product.

- The addition of risky ventures – some very risky ventures with potentially high profits may be considered if the portfolio contains enough stable, albeit less profitable ventures.

- Liquidation – avoiding risk by opting for a known outcome, rather than banking on an unstable business with an uncertain future. Generally speaking, however, survival is usually preferred to liquidation, even though the latter is less risky.

- Hedging against cyclical risks – manufacturing swimwear or tennis rackets in one business unit and skiing gear in another, for example.

- Forward and backward vertical integration in industries not subject to sudden environmental changes in order to reduce the risks associated with dependence upon certain suppliers, distributors, and so on.

For decades, financial planners and managers all over the world have been stressing that risk is just as fundamental a consideration of a given investment as are the projected profits. The element of risk has always been a crucial consideration when compiling an investment portfolio, that is, in deciding 'what and when to buy or sell'.

Line managers and business planners in commercial and industrial firms, however, have frequently made decisions regarding which product lines or markets to expand or contract, add or delete from the business portfolio, on the basis of expected profits and cash flow, disregarding explicit treatment of risk. This simplistic approach is viewed as imprudent and has even cost many companies their lives.

Financially, investment in a business unit is not conceptually different from investment in stocks or bonds, with all its attendant risk. Approval of an investment in a given product line without giving the proper attention to the risk involved is a gross oversight.

Managing a business portfolio, however, is fundamentally different from managing a portfolio of securities, which can be bought or sold at a moment's notice[1] by a simple telephone call. Buying and selling businesses entails changing organizations, hiring and firing personnel, selling and acquiring machinery, buildings, production licenses – the list is endless. It could also mean dispersing or accumulating a great deal of knowledge – technical, managerial, professional, and so on. Each and every one of these elements must be considered in real terms at the business level, in order to assess the overall risk the SBU faces, and to enable a comparison of SBUs in completely different industries.

What is risk?

Risk is a term with a multitude of definitions, however universal the meaning of the concept. Considering risk basically means trying to estimate expectancy: the range of possible outcomes, together with their probabilities. Risk is commonly described as calculated. This means that a person or company knows that a certain event may happen, with particular results. There is an estimated probability that this event, rather than other possibilities, will in fact take place. Risk at the business level will include risks related to marketing, to R&D, to production, to distribution, and so on. We have mentioned that in the past many managers defined success as the achievement of an expected return on investment of 15%, and calculated financial risk only. This concept has become inadequate, as shown by the life-cycle approach: high risks must be taken if Question Marks are to be changed into Stars, whereas risks related to Milking Cows are low by comparison.

It has been said that 'to try to eliminate risk in business is futile. The main goal of management science must be to enable business to take the right risk.'[2] The right risk, of course, is not easily defined.

Definitions

Risky situation

Once defined as 'both uncertainty and the results of uncertainty',[3] a risky situation has come to be referred to as one in which the outcome is subject to an uncontrollable random event, stemming from a known probability distribution. An uncertain situation by contrast is one in which the outcome is subject to an uncontrollable random event stemming from an unknown probability distribution.[4]

Known probability

A known probability distribution in this case means that the distribution can be estimated by an educated guess or calculated on the basis of past experience regarding frequencies of similar events. Uncertainty, on the other hand, means that we cannot calculate or estimate the probability of occurrence for the various possible events.

Defining risk

Risk, though interpreted differently over the course of time, has frequently been incorporated into the analysis of business portfolios. It has, however, usually been narrowly defined in terms of the variance of cash flow and return on investment. Some researchers treat risk as random variability in any relevant variable. This leads us to the understanding that risk may be incorporated into any model in which there is a probability distribution of deviation from an expected value. If this definition is acceptable, then risk may be incorporated into any number of models which may or may not include variation in return on investment. In this case, a more suitable definition of risk is that 'variation in a variable is itself a variable', and of course that variable must be defined.

Assessing risk

In the simplest case, when one does not possess more complete information on a risk variable – such as variance in sales levels, prices or costs – the 'most likely' value is assumed. This value is then used throughout the decision-making process and is assumed to be correct. Note that this method, though widely used, entails inaccuracy, misjudgment and bias. It is basically guessing by a gut feeling of the decision maker. Its main advantage is that it saves time and money in searching for data.

There are several methods for assessing risk in a more systematic manner:

- **Past experience**
  The method of trying to predict the future on the basis of past events is reliable only if the company has substantial experience with the specific type of event (using the law of large numbers in statistics), under conditions that are likely to apply in the future. Hertz[5] notes, in his introduction to risk in strategic decision making, that risk analysis itself does not eliminate uncertainty. It can, however, represent the average outcome for similar decisions that have been made numerous times in the past.

- **Experience of others**
  If the firm has little experience but can acquire data pertaining to the experience of other firms, this data may be aggregated to assess risks. The value may be developed in consultation with experts in the field. Extreme care must be exercised in these cases, as we do not actually know what will ultimately happen in the future. It is generally accepted that experts tend to be overly pessimistic judges in short-range planning, and overly optimistic in long-range planning. The optimism or pessimism of specialists can and should be taken into consideration when making decision based on their judgment.

- **Simulation of future scenarios**
  This is yet another method for assessing the risk related to competitive actions. It takes the form of simulation games, where the experts act as decision makers in the computerized or role-playing game, and actions

are based on these experts' opinions of what the future holds in store and on their evaluation of competitive options and strategies.

Risk in previously-discussed models

Several of the previously discussed models of portfolio analysis, in their original forms, have been strongly criticized for their lack of attention to the risk element. Examples include the BCG and DPM models (*see* previous chapters). When used by themselves, these models lack the risk dimension, so crucial to a comprehensive appraisal of any product portfolio. In the research literature, most attempts to elaborate on the risk dimension have been extensions of the classical portfolio models, rather than the development of new concepts.

BCG

The BCG model does not handle risk in an explicit manner at the business level, although it does address risk indirectly at the corporate level.[6] According to the BCG approach, there must be a balance between the degree of risk and the profit expectations of the corporation. For example, companies in mature markets will probably try to shift investment into newer growth fields.[7]

Thus at the corporate level the cash-flow shift does not have to be perfectly balanced at all times. Depending on the corporation's preferred level of financial risk, excess funds may be invested as they become available, and long-term bonds or stock may be issued to raise external funding.

Among the variations of the BCG model, that devised by the Mead Corporation should be mentioned. Not satisfied with the names given by BCG (after all, who wants to be a manager of Dogs?), they acknowledged the importance of risk by proposing other names that imply the various levels of risk: Sweepstake for Question Marks, Savings Account for Stars, Bonds for Cash Cows, and Mortgage for Dogs. They also elaborated upon the risk level innate to each cell: Sweepstake – extremely high risk, Savings Account – medium risk, Bond – low risk, Mortgage – medium risk.[8]

GE/McKinsey

The GE matrix addresses risk only partially – there is mention of risk in some (but not all) strategic options within the matrix cells – particularly the losing business-level strategies defined as being 'in the red'. For example,

Loser 1. (medium industry attractiveness, low business strength) has a variety of options, including 'locate possibilities of expanding areas of low risk'. The matrix does not specify how the Winners 'in the green' should handle risk.

Hosmer[9] expanded the concepts of the GE/McKinsey matrix by elaborating a direct relationship of the GE/McKinsey model to the life-cycle approach. He notes that the three major investment categories – 'invest', 'maintain' and 'divest' – relate directly to the three major stages of the life cycle, respectively – 'Development & Growth', 'Shakeout & Maturity', 'Saturation & Decline'.

Hosmer notes that McKinsey has an explicit list of recommendations for each category, which include the risk levels recommended for each stage. When an invest for growth strategy is adopted, the inherent risk is accepted and attempts should be made to contain it. In the case of an SBU selected for a maintenance strategy, the objective is to limit risk. When the decision is taken to divest an SBU, management should avoid all risk during the disposal process.

Without explicitly saying so, Hosmer has shown that there are different types of risk in business strategies, other than financial risks. His suggested measures also include the variable of management's attitude towards risk.[9]

DPM

The DPM model is the basis of the Risk Matrix developed by Hussey, and will be discussed later in detail. Suffice it to say at this point that the lack of treatment of risk in this model and others inspired Hussey to develop a more comprehensive business portfolio model.

Hofer–Schendel

Hofer and Schendel do not explicitly identify the risk for each strategy. This is understandable, since each of their generic strategies covers a number of adjacent cells in the matrix, even though the competitive risks are bound to be different for strong, average and weak SBUs. This is one of the drawbacks of the generality of their business-level strategic guidelines. However, they do mention risk in several contexts.

- **Corporate level risk**
  Corporate level risk consists of financial and market risk. Financial risk refers to the risk associated with the ability to meet short-term financial obligations. Market risk is the risk involved in investing in markets in order to improve competitive position. The two types of risk are

interrelated. Total corporate risk is the sum of its financial and market risk. Risk levels vary for different types of portfolios: for example, profit portfolios tend to have lower levels of financial risk than growth portfolios, while the opposite is true with regard to market risk.[10]

- **Business-level risk**
  Risk can be partially assessed by anticipating the reactions of competitors to the chosen SBU strategies. In other words, competitor analysis should be used in evaluating several possible scenarios for a given strategy. For example, one scenario could be given in which the competitor does not react, another in which it retaliates strongly, and so on. This concept of combining competitor analysis with risk analysis is unique to Hofer and Schendel's model.

ADL

The original ADL approach relates to the risk element as one of the last steps in the planning process. This stage of the analysis involves estimating the risk level of the strategy chosen for each SBU. Using this approach, risk is analyzed after business strategies are formulated, not in parallel. Risk is defined by ADL in terms of the predictability of profit performance: the more unpredictable, the higher the risk.

ADL assesses risk by the following eight variables, which can be rated high, medium or low:

- **Risk associated with maturity and competitive position**
  This is assessed directly as the position of the unit within the life-cycle matrix. Newer and/or weaker SBUs are associated with higher risk than their older and stronger counterparts.

- **Risk inherent in the industry**
  Some industries are just plain riskier than others (high fashion vs. ready-to-wear clothing).

- **Risk inherent in the strategy**
  Major increases in marketing communication expenditures, for example, may or may not lead to market share increase.

- **Risk related to accuracy of assumptions about the future**

- **Risk related to past performance of unit**
  It is likely that SBUs that have successfully implemented new strategies in the past will be more likely to continue to do so than SBUs that do not have such a record.

- **Risk related to past performance of management**

- **Risk related to performance improvement**
  Performance improvement is defined as the gap between existing and expected performance: the larger the gap, the greater the risk involved.

An overall risk profile is thus calculated for the strategy under analysis. To date, this is the most comprehensive list of business risk factors that are not strictly financial factors.

Congruence tests

ADL has a comprehensive list of so-called congruence tests. The original purpose of these tests was to predict whether the chosen strategy has a fair chance of succeeding, given the specific circumstances of the particular SBU under consideration. We take this idea one step further: the congruence tests could very well be used as a tool for measuring risk for each and every factor on the list. For example, if we are examining the organizational feasibility of a strategy, we will be examining whether the organization is open enough to accept the strategy, and whether the manager is of the right type to carry it through. We will be checking whether there is good congruence among the many operational factors that are critical success factors. Good congruence implies low risk, and poor congruence implies high risk, for the specific factor. This is a nonfinancial tool for assessing risk, and it is one possible interpretation of the ADL congruence tests.[11, 12]

The three-dimensional matrix: Hussey's Risk Matrix (RM)

Introduction

Shell Chemicals' 1975 development of the Directional Policy Matrix (DPM) led to a general technique that applies to virtually any diversified business containing distinct and identifiable SBUs. Like the Growth Share Matrix of The Boston Consulting Group, which created a stir within America's corporate planning community, the DPM applications created a stir within the decision makers' community, particularly in capital-intensive industries.

This method of strategic decision making was a revolutionary concept in the petrochemical industry, where it was first conceived of by Shell.

As discussed in detail in Chapter 4, the horizontal axis of the DPM depicts the competitive position and the vertical axis represents market sector profitability of the SBU being analyzed. This illustration by Hussey is actually a transposition of the original DPM matrix. Each SBU is scored according to the relative appraisal of these two factors and positioned on the grid. The risk is assessed for each SBU and reviewed simultaneously with the other two axes.

Applications of the DPM model were discussed in detail by Hussey in his 1978 article 'Portfolio Analysis: Practical Experience with the Directional Policy Matrix'.[13] In documenting uses of the model within the Rolls-Royce Motor Company and the National Freight Corporation, Hussey's ultimate aim was to achieve both validity – the ability to measure what we set out to measure – and reliability – the quality of consistency of the model. The general concept behind the technique was to let the decision makers in the corporation analyze, agree upon and construct many of the basic assumptions, such as which environmental factors play an important role, or whether different sectors should have different scales for measuring market growth rate. Hussey discovered, however, that neither of his two aims was fully achieved. Some reliability was achieved, in that certain independent groups reached the same conclusions. Still, whereas with the Rolls-Royce Motor Company the model was sufficient for conservative analysis, the National Freight Corporation required a much more sophisticated analysis, coupling the model with a risk analysis matrix, in order to maintain a variable level of risk. It is along these lines that Hussey developed the Risk Matrix portfolio application.

Ultimately he applied the full Risk Matrix technique to his study of the National Freight Corporation. In his comprehensive study of Rolls-Royce, however, the Risk Matrix was used for exploration purposes only, the outcome being presented as a standard two-dimensional matrix.

Hussey's Risk Matrix (RM) is utilized to assess the significant external influences on a particular business, and the consequences of adverse affects on the product portfolio, including the probability of these adverse effects actually occurring. In his 1978 article, he essentially added a third dimension – the environmental risk axis – to the previously existing two-dimensional Directional Policy Matrix.

The planning focus: Adding risk

The objective of the Risk Matrix model is the creation and maintenance of a portfolio of businesses that earn an acceptable rate of return in accordance with the level of risk they encounter. At the corporate level, the approach allows the corporation to spread risk across the portfolio. At the level of the SBU, the model focuses upon the attainment of a return that is commensurate with the inherent level of risk. Acceptable ratios of risk and return are dictated by stakeholders.

Dimensions X, Y, Z

Hussey built his Risk Matrix on the Directional Policy Matrix, utilizing similar definitions for the Market Sector Profitability and Competitive Position axes. Essentially, Hussey first built two two-dimensional matrices:

risk vs. market sector profitability and market sector profitability vs. competitive position (the DPM). He then converted them into a three-dimensional matrix, with risk on the third (Z) axis.

3D grid

We shall assume that the reader is now well acquainted with the X and Y axes of the DPM model, and will not repeat them here in the representation of the risk matrix.

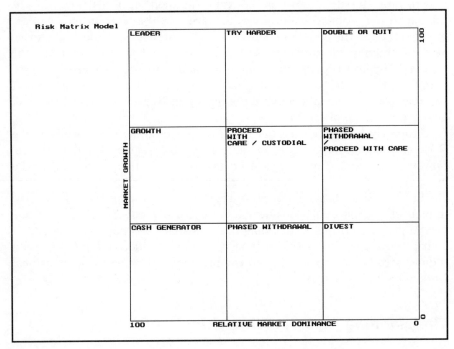

Figure 7.1   Risk matrix model.

The nine cells of the first two dimensions are almost identical to those of DPM. They include: Leader, Try Harder, Double or Quit, Growth, Proceed with Care, Cash Generator, Phased Withdrawal (x2) and Divest. Hussey's Proceed with Care is essentially the same as the DPM Custodial. Only the name was changed, as it did not suit the concepts of the original client of the RM. Another client preferred to name it Keep/Watch.

Calculating risk

Hussey defines risk as any factor or event in the environment that may have an adverse affect on an SBU. Risk is an increasing function of two components: the impact of the adverse event, should it occur, and the estimated probability that it will actually occur.

According to Hussey the element of environmental risk – which is out of the company's control – is a factor to be considered during all strategic planning stages. Risk is a vital factor in an SBU's external environment, as it pertains to competitors, customers, ultimate potential, and numerous other critical success factors. Hussey emphasizes that the element of risk must be considered in relation to all components of the environment, and not solely in terms of financial risk. However, one must not overlook the diverse nature of environmental factors, as different levels of risk are imposed on different types of businesses, depending on the particular environmental circumstances. In other words – though all businesses are exposed to external influences, the impact differs.

Hussey suggested that risk be analyzed for a number of crucial environmental factors. His first step in the analysis is to identify the primary environmental factors that impose external risk on the SBU. After compiling a list of factors, the risk level of – each factor is assessed.

These levels of risk are assessed by two sub-factors:

- The impact that an adverse change (in the environment) will have on the SBU.

- The probability that these adverse changes may actually occur.

In other words, risk is assessed so that if an adverse change in the environment will have a drastic effect on the SBU under consideration, and the probability of this change occurring is high, then the environmental risk is high for this SBU.

Hussey had originally introduced four major levels of relative risk impact and assigned each level a score as follows:

Extremely High	6
High	4
Relatively low	2
None	0
(Note: Intermediate or 'odd number' impact scores also exist.)	

Accordingly, he drew up a table of probabilities, to translate estimates such as 'very likely to happen' into a point on a nominal scale of 0%–100%, and specified a score for each probability:

Described likelihood	Probability scale	Probability score
A certainty	100%	6
Very likely	84%	5
Quite possible	67%	4
As likely as not	50%	3
Probably not	33%	2
Highly unlikely	16%	1
Impossible or highly improbable	0%	0

The inherent risk of an environmental factor is calculated by multiplying its impact score by its probability score: Minimum 0(0×0), Maximum 36(6×6). The overall risk of an SBU is the sum of the risk of all relevant factors. The sums are normalized, and the result is a risk score for each SBU, which is entered on the third dimension of the RM.

We discovered that Hussey's method of calculating risk results in much confusion. Managers have difficulty in identifying environmental factors, and assessing their impact and probability of occurrence. Thus in this book we measure risk differently: we adopt the definition of risk which interprets it as the variability of a relevant variable. In order to assess risk, we calculate the variance of an SBU's expected RONA (return on net assets) by using a method and an equation that approximate the variance of a beta distribution.[14] The assessment requires that management, by means of educated guesses, estimate optimistic and pessimistic values for RONA for the next year. On the basis of many implementations, we believe that this method eliminates much of the confusion associated with Hussey's method of risk calculation, as the number of estimated variables is greatly reduced and the estimation of the variables is easier and more accurate.

The SBUs are then depicted in the three-dimensional matrix (cube), where risk is the third Z dimension.

Relevant strategic variables

To use Hussey's risk matrix, values for the following variables should be assigned.

Risk (Z axis)	Business strength variables (X axis)	Market attractiveness variables (Y axis)
Risk RONA variance	Relative market share	Market growth rate
Optimistic RONA next year	Distribution network coverage	Relative industry profitability
Pessimistic RONA next year	Distribution network effectiveness	Customer value
	Technology skills	Customer brand loyalty
	Flexibility	Technological barriers to entry
	Production efficiency	
	Experience-curve	Customer/manufacturer bargaining power
	Feedstock	Product substitutability
	Product quality	Generation of after-sales business
	R&D	
	Economies of scale	Industry's capacity for response
	After-sales service	

The following are the definitions and measures of the new variables not defined in the previous chapters.

Risk (Z axis)

Optimistic RONA – next year

Definition: A high RONA estimate for the next year of activity that will occur only under rare favorable conditions. There is very little chance (say 1 in 100) of reaching an RONA higher than this optimistic RONA.

Measurement: RONA is measured in percent of net profit after taxes of net assets.

Pessimistic RONA – next year

Definition: A low RONA estimate for the next year of activity that will occur only under rare unfavorable conditions. There is very little chance (say 1 in 100) of reaching an RONA lower than this pessimistic RONA.

Measurement: RONA is measured in percent of net profit after taxes of net assets.

Risk RONA variance

Definition: The variances of the RONA estimates for the next year of activity:

$$(\text{Optimistic RONA next year} - \text{Pessimistic RONA next year})^2/6$$

Use of the model

The Risk Matrix is used to systematically explore and examine key environmental factors and their potential influence upon individual SBUs and the corporate portfolio as a whole. The approach enables management to include these factors in the strategic decision-making process and to anticipate the possible outcomes of a chosen strategy.

A competitor's reaction is an external variable of great potential impact. The Risk Matrix can be utilized to generate scenarios of risk related to competitor behavior. A competitor analysis using RM is more difficult, as estimating the impact of adverse changes on a competitor requires intimate knowledge of its position and strategy.

Hussey also suggests that the three-dimensional matrix concept be used to analyze the portfolio chosen by the corporation against specific problems the strategy may encounter, such as vulnerability to inflation, energy consumption, capital needs, and so on.

Basic assumptions

Hussey's basic assumption in his Risk Matrix is that 'all businesses are subjected to influences outside the control of the company, but some are more affected than others.' These influences must be considered and evaluated.

Taking Hussey's RM model one step further, we claim that management, in order to properly assess the business portfolio, must be able to properly assess environmental risk. The model and Hussey's definitions contain the underlying assumption that there is a degree of uncertainty in any environmental factor, which must be taken into account whenever one is dealing with future events.

A basic problem in portfolio analysis, according to Hussey, is agreeing upon the scale of market growth rate to be used for analyzing the assorted businesses in the portfolio. One possibility is to use a different scale for each business sector, based upon the average growth rate within each industry. The other possibility – the one Hussey recommends – is to use as a benchmark an average of the growth rates of all the industries the corporation is assessing.

Thus Hussey makes a contribution to the coherent use of the DPM, even before introducing and treating the third axis – the risk axis.

Limits, critique, and misuse

It is important to recognize that use of the RM model in corporate portfolio planning should not be perceived as a magic button which at a touch will supply the corporation with answers on what to do. It is important to realize that it should not be used on its own, but rather in conjunction with other techniques and models in order to provide a logical and comprehensive analysis.

Hussey discusses a comprehensive list of practical problems that arise in using the RM:

- Should different criteria be applied in evaluating different businesses?

- How extensive should the list of variables be?

- Should all variables be weighted equally? Hussey's answer is that if they are not equally weighted, then they may not be comparable.

    He does not have a definite opinion on this issue. In order to assess the impact of different sets of weights on the result, we recommend that the executive or student try at least two sets of identical variables for two SBUs – one set with identical weights and the other with weights that vary for different markets.

- The elimination of variables can distort calculations. Hussey, therefore, recommends not to eliminate them when they appear to be less relevant, but to rate them with lower importance scores.

- As in many of the other models, the problem of defining the market arises. Hussey cautions that this definition may be dynamic, and needs to be re-evaluated periodically.

A possible misuse pointed out by Hussey is likely to occur when divestment strategy is chosen for an SBU that shares a joint resource – such as production facilities – with another SBU. Hussey duly notes that, unless the excess capacity can be diverted to a more profitable activity, the divestment may cause additional complications.

There are several pitfalls in estimating or assessing risk values:

- Rates of inflation are difficult to forecast for long-range planning.

- Foreign exchange rates are difficult to forecast for long-range planning.

- Changes in government regulations may be a major source of uncertainty.

Hussey also warns that some portfolio analysis techniques tend to rule out strategies of small-share producers in certain markets, even though these may be very profitable. The techniques can be used to define a valid strategy, but should not be used to rationalize for poor performance.

Another shortcoming of the approach is that Hussey does not indicate what a 'balanced cube' (portfolio) should include, nor does he say which type of SBUs should be taking the risk – strong ones in all sectors or weak ones in high-profit sectors. There are no guidelines as to optimal movements within the cube, or how risk should be used to decide on 'Double or Quit'.

Hussey provides us with a simple yet strong tool for assessing risk at the business level, but leaves us empty-handed at the corporate level. We can only assume what was true for other models: the level of risk to be taken, that is, what would be considered an acceptable rate of return for a given level of risk, or what would be an acceptable level of risk for a given rate of return, is dictated by the stakeholders.

8

The risk–return model

Introduction

In the previous chapter we 'ate the cake and still had it': we incorporated risk into the portfolio matrix, and still kept the basic structure, at least in two of its dimensions. While the Hussey approach to risk is consistent with the traditional portfolio matrix presentation, in the present chapter we venture into new territory. The risk–return approach is very conclusive; instead of evaluating many measures which affect performance, it focuses on a single end result – the SBU's profitability. True, the method calls for evaluation of profitability, that is, return on net assets, under different states of nature, but the focus is on this variable alone. Unlike other portfolio approaches which try to refine evaluation by breaking forecasts down into components, here we lump-sum all the measures into a single one: profitability.

History: Development and use

For many years now, economists and financial managers have been using the risk–return approach to evaluate the performance of a portfolio of securities and stocks. More recently, Cardozo and Wind[1] suggested that a similar tool may be used for evaluating the performance of businesses and products. In this book we will concentrate on evaluating the performance of portfolios comprised of SBUs, briefly discussing the evaluation of product lines in the 'additions and variations' section.

In contrast to the models described in previous chapters, which aimed at balancing cash flows, or increasing return on investment, the Cardozo–Wind model aims to increase the productivity (defined below) of SBU investments. In addition, most of the previously discussed models used the dimensions of business strength and industry attractiveness for portfolio design and strategic planning; the Cardozo–Wind model utilizes risk and return as the basic criteria for mapping and evaluating the business portfolio. Its main use is to evaluate the productivity of a current portfolio of businesses, assess future scenarios, and finally, evaluate possible additions and deletions of SBUs from the portfolio.

The basic premise of the model is that whereas all managers strive to maximize the productivity of their portfolios of SBUs, each has his/her personal approach to risk. Therefore, the level of risk each manager is willing to undertake may be different. The principle of the model is that for every degree of risk an SBU manager takes, there is a specific level of expected return. The most productive set of businesses that the corporation is involved with at a particular time forms an 'efficient frontier' (EF). The EF is a useful benchmark or criterion for deciding on adding new businesses via mergers, acquisitions and internal development, or on dropping unsuccessful businesses. Another useful criterion is the hurdle rate – a specific level of expected return which is a minimum requirement for management to embark on a particular investment.

One of the main contributions of the Cardozo–Wind model is that it explicitly deals with new and potential SBUs. Some of the other strategic planning models, by the very nature of the measures they utilize, assume that the markets and the businesses already exist, and are more or less fully developed, and thus unintentionally 'ignore' start-ups.

Another contribution and distinction of this model is that the manager deals explicitly with the future, and evaluates possible strategies by projecting future outcomes. Many of the previously discussed models basically assist the manager in evaluating past and present performance and lay down rather general guidelines for future strategies. The Cardozo–Wind model compels the manager to think out the future in detail. Cardozo and Wind describe one real-world application of their model to a specific corporation, fictitiously named Monitrol. This corporation had four business units, all involved in highly technical, but different markets. While this is the only example given, it may well be one of several or even many actual applications. The reader is referred to Cardozo and Wind's original article (1985) for fuller details.

The planning focus: RISK/ROI

Productivity of a business unit is defined as the return received for a given level of accepted risk or, alternatively, the risk associated with a given level of expected return. The goal, according to Cardozo and Wind, is to maximize productivity. At the business level, this means maximizing the expected return for a given level of accepted risk, or minimizing the risk for a given level of expected return, for an SBU. At the corporate level, the objective is to choose an efficient set of SBUs.

Cardozo and Wind use these two criteria – risk and return – as the basis for deciding on investments, divestments, and reallocation of resources among SBUs. The third criterion is the corporate hurdle rate, which will be defined below.

As is the case with a portfolio of securities and stocks, a business portfolio (or a portfolio of SBUs) consists of businesses with a range of low to high expected returns, on the one hand, and low to high risk levels, on the other. The SBUs are depicted on a two-dimensional graph which displays the return as a function of risk. This function will be different for different corporations. The Risk–Return Chart is the basic tool of the Cardozo–Wind model. A third criterion for strategic decision making, the hurdle rate, is a specific rate of return that serves as a go/no-go benchmark for decision making. Any business that produces a rate of return under the hurdle rate defined by management is discarded, and those that fall on or above the hurdle rate are appropriate for further consideration. The hurdle rate is a single-dimensional criterion, examining only one variable – return (*see also* Critique and Misuse).

Use and display of the matrix

Dimensions

Each of the two dimensions on the risk–return graph consists of a single variable. The Y (vertical) axis depicts the expected level of return.

Cardozo and Wind define return as follows:

$$\frac{\text{after tax operating profit} + \text{non-cash charges}}{\text{net fixed assets} + \text{current assets used to generate those returns}}$$

In this book we will define return as RONA, already described in Chapter 2.

Calculating SBU return

In the original Cardozo–Wind approach return is forecasted by management for a number of possible SBU environments. Next, the probability that each given environment will indeed prevail is evaluated. The expected return for an environment weighted by the probability of its occurrence is the average expected return. An SBU's expected level of return is its weighted average return or the sum of average expected returns for all environments considered.

In this book, we suggest a somewhat simplified approach, whereby return is the expected return (RONA), the weighted average return of three scenarios facing the SBU – an optimistic, a pessimistic and a most likely outcome. The X (horizontal) axis depicts the risk level.

We note at this point that Cardozo and Wind's definition of risk is different from that used in the models discussed in previous chapters. In the previous models risk was defined as uncertainty, likelihood of loss, danger or downside risk, and estimated by one of several heuristic or statistical methods used in decision theory.[2] Cardozo and Wind define risk, in accordance with accepted practices for securities portfolios,[3] on the basis of the variance in return. The greater the potential fluctuation of return around the expected level of return, the riskier is the investment. Thus risk includes upside as well as downside variations. Risk is calculated directly from the various scenarios predicted for existing or proposed SBUs.

In the original Cardozo and Wind approach the X-axis is calculated as the sum of the squared deviations from the estimated return for each and every SBU, weighted by the probability of occurrence of each environment. Variation may result from several sets of environmental conditions or from measurements at different points in time. The period-to-period changes in strategies and/or environmental conditions lead to variations in return along time periods.

In this book we calculate risk as described in the previous chapter, using optimistic and pessimistic values of RONA to calculate the standard deviation.

Corporate return and risk

Corporate return is the average of returns for each SBU in the portfolio, weighted by the SBU's relative assets. Overall corporate risk is the sum of each SBU's risk weighted by its relative assets.

Grid

After calculating its expected return and risk characteristics, each SBU is plotted on the two-dimensional risk–return graph shown in Figure 8.1. A line is drawn through the points that have the highest and/or most leftward values, that is, the highest return for a given level of risk (SBU d vs. SBU f) or the lowest risk for a given return rate (SBU b vs. SBU f).

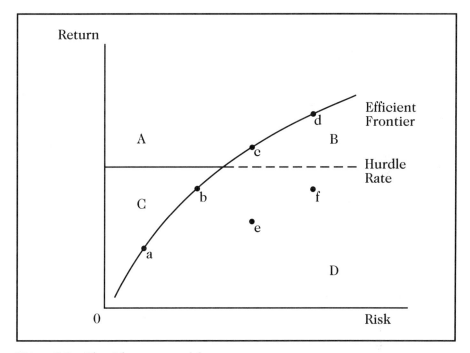

Figure 8.1 The risk–return model.

Source: *Long Range Planning*, 18, Cardozo, R. N. and Wind, J. "Risk return approach to product portfolio strategy", pages 78–9, Copyright 1985, with kind permission from Elsevier Science Ltd., The Boulevard, Langford Lane, Kidlington, OX5 1GB, U.K.

The line depicted on the graph is the efficient frontier of the specific corporation under examination at a specific point in time. The hurdle rate is then added to the graph. This is an additional go/no-go criterion: SBUs that fall under a specific return rate are automatically rejected. With this third criterion, the risk–return graph is now divided into four areas or cells: A, B, C, & D.

Cell A

SBUs in Cell A are new SBUs, as they are above the current efficient frontier. SBUs in Cell A are characterized by high returns for lower risks than those that comprise the current efficient frontier. Cell A is not square; the extension at the upper right-hand side of the cell has exceptionally high expected returns, for higher-risk SBUs. In BCG terms, these are often the Question Marks that the corporation might be able to turn into Stars by adopting radically new strategies. Such risks are usually accepted if management is comprised of high-risk takers.

Cell B

SBUs in Cell B have relatively low returns for high risks. Such SBUs are candidates for rejection, as their high risk levels place them under the efficient frontier, even though they are above the hurdle rate for return.

Cell C

SBUs in Cell C are characterized by positive returns for low risks, and would be accepted if the efficient frontier was the sole criterion. This, however, is not the case. SBUs in Cell C are candidates for rejection, since they fall under the hurdle rate, and thus do not meet the minimum return requirements of the corporation.

Cell D

SBUs in Cell D are prime candidates for rejection, as they fall under the efficient frontier and have returns that are lower than the corporate hurdle rate. Thus their small expected contributions are added at the expense of relatively high increases in the overall risk assumed by the corporation.

Relevant strategic variables

To use the risk–return approach, values for the following variables should be assigned:

- Expected RONA next year,
- Risk-RONA variance,
- Most likely RONA next year,
- Optimistic RONA next year,
- Pessimistic RONA next year.

Following are the definitions and measurements of the new variables not defined in the previous chapters.

Expected RONA next year

> **Definition:** Expected return on net assets for next year of activity. It is an RONA estimate with a 50-50 chance of being over- or underachieved. The mean RONA for next year is:

> ((Most likely RONA next year)×4 + Optimistic RONA next year + Pessimistic RONA next year)/6

Most likely RONA next year

> **Definition:** The best single educated guess of the return on net assets for the next year of activity.

Use of the model

The Cardozo–Wind model can be used at two strategic levels: the corporate level and the business level. Given the focus of this book, we will concentrate on the corporate level. The risk–return graph may, however, also be used at the business level, for product-line decisions within an SBU (*see* 'Additions' section).

Corporate portfolio balancing

The main use of the model at the corporate level is as a guide for mergers and acquisitions, investments and divestments of SBUs. The objective is to choose the most productive set of business units. The productivity of a set of SBUs is determined by the weighted expected average return and risk of the SBUs that comprise the set. Different sets of SBUs may form different efficient frontiers. These sets may well have higher expected returns and lower overall risks than the sum of the individual SBUs that comprise them, in cases where advantage is taken of favorable covariances among the SBUs in choosing the sets. This procedure is equivalent to measuring covariance in a securities and stocks portfolio, but is much simpler: no covariance combinations are necessary for calculating the portfolio productivity, as the favorable advantages are 'built into' the SBU evaluations at the scenario-planning stage.

SBUs that fall below and to the right of the efficient frontier can be removed to increase the productivity of the portfolio. In cases where they cannot be removed, the resources allocated to them should be reduced.

Low-productivity SBUs should be removed only if the resources can be invested more productively elsewhere.

Choosing the most productive set of businesses is a four-step procedure, which includes:

1. Defining the SBUs

Managerial judgment is exercised in defining the SBUs, based on the criteria of commonality of demand and market forces. This commonality of course is based on previous analyses of market structure and demand–resource interdependence.

2. Evaluating SBUs

This step involves identifying the relevant scenarios for each SBU and estimating the expected return and probabilities of occurrence for each scenario.

The input data for measuring portfolio productivity includes a list of all the possible investments, and a construction of the corporation's efficient frontier on a risk–return graph. 'What if' sensitivity analysis for different sets would entail including or excluding some of the existing and planned SBUs.

The calculation of return and risk for each SBU is performed on the basis of the following inputs:

- Projections on the basis of historical performance,

- Forecasts of new product performance,

- Environmental analysis, that is, scenario construction,

- Identification of driving forces of scenarios,

- Assessment of likelihood of occurrence and impact of driving forces.

Management should estimate the range of returns and specify the conditions under which the high/low returns will occur. This will help identify opportunities.

All the SBUs should be plotted in such a way that less efficient ones may be identified, and considered for divestment. The efficient frontier is the main criterion for deciding on new SBUs in the Cardozo–Wind model. Any proposed SBU must have its return and risk rates calculated, so that it can be plotted on the risk–return graph with the existing SBUs. If it falls close to the efficient frontier it should be considered as a viable option. An SBU falling above and to the left of the efficient frontier should be given favorable consideration as it may afford the corporation a chance to 'move' and thus improve its efficient frontier, and gain a more productive set of businesses. If the proposed SBU falls to the right and under the efficient frontier, it should be dropped from further analysis.

3. Measuring portfolio productivity

Productivity at the corporate level is gauged by calculating the weighted expected average return and risk of all the SBUs combined. This initial measurement acts as a benchmark for decision making with regard to the composition of the corporate portfolio. All investment or divestment decisions should increase productivity by improving the return commensurate with a given level of risk or by lowering the risk for a given level of return.

4. Selecting from among sets of investments

At this point, it is important to note how management's personal attitude towards risk enters into portfolio planning.

Let us say that two SBUs are being considered, only one of which will be chosen, and that both fall in Area A. One has a low return and is less risky, the other has a high return but is highly risky. As both will increase the overall productivity of the portfolio, management may choose either, depending on their personal utility functions. Risk averters may choose the former option, whereas risk takers may choose the latter.

Guidelines for Aligning 'Choice of SBU Set' with Long-Term Objectives

There are three general methods of choosing the portfolio set:

1. Choose the lower part of the efficient frontier if one of the objectives is to avoid the possibility of large losses.

2. Choose the upper part of the efficient frontier if one of the objectives is to maximize returns, and management is willing to accept high variance in returns (that is, high risk).

3. Choose from both ends or from the middle of the efficient frontier if a balanced portfolio is desired.

Assumptions, critique, limitations and misuse

The Cardozo–Wind Model is based on the assumption that the criteria for investing or divesting in securities and stocks portfolios are adequate and appropriate for investing/divesting in business portfolios, that is, risk and return are totally and completely adequate. There is, however, one major difference. Whereas low-productivity stock should be removed from a securities and stocks portfolio (since ample investment opportunities are usually available), low-productivity SBUs can be removed from a business portfolio only if the resources can be invested more productively elsewhere.

Other underlying assumptions of the model are that return is directly related to risk – higher expected return is associated with higher risk and vice versa – and that business investments have the same objectives as securities and stocks investments.

Analyzing SBUs from a purely financial point of view has its benefits, in that, as Cardozo and Wind state, such an analysis 'bases the portfolio on managers' objectives'. In our opinion, this statement is only partially correct, as it takes into consideration only return objectives (and consequently risk objectives). If, for example, one of the corporate objectives (related to long-term goals and strategies) is to be a technological leader in a certain field, this will not be considered in the Cardozo–Wind model. Another example would be the rivalry between two SBUs of the following nature: a small investment that falls on the efficient frontier, versus a large investment that falls short of the efficient frontier. The large SBU adds substantial revenues to the corporation, provides many jobs, and so on, whereas the small SBU contributes marginal revenues, provides few jobs, and so on. This model should therefore not be used on its own, but in conjunction with other models, which consider other, nonfinancial criteria.

Using the hurdle rate has its limitations. The hurdle rate may eliminate a large part of the lower left-hand side of the efficient frontier (based on the specific efficient frontier and the specific hurdle rate of the corporation). As a result, the range of SBUs that fall within the relevant combinations may be narrowed down considerably, and may hamper the design of a well-balanced portfolio. Start-up businesses are characterized by very low return rates in the short and intermediate term, and if the hurdle rate is set too high, the corporation may remain without future Stars. Another element that Cardozo and Wind have ignored is the effect a manager has on the return rate in a business portfolio. The SBU manager can have a direct impact, causing increases or decreases in the SBU's return, whereas the securities and stocks portfolio manager has much less influence on the outcome of a specific investment. This is a major difference that the Cardozo–Wind model overlooks.

Cardozo and Wind have adopted an elaborate approach to the definition of SBUs. How should one handle an SBU that has, for example, five product–market groups, each having, let's say, three possible future environment-scenarios? Cardozo and Wind solved the complications of hundreds (even thousands) of possibilities and calculations by their definition of an SBU, according to which product–market investments are grouped into SBUs by commonality of demand.

Product–market groups that are affected by the same market forces may be considered simultaneously for calculation purposes. Complementary and competing products are therefore included in the same SBU. Separate SBUs are independent and therefore covariance need not be estimated. This definition is identical in meaning to the definition of an SBU used throughout this book.

The Cardozo–Wind model seems to view the corporation in a vacuum, setting it in an unreal sort of environment. Its two variables do not seem to cover all the elements in the environment. Even so, it is a very powerful tool for evaluating the financial aspect of business portfolios, and is extremely valuable for assessing new products and forecasting their performance.

A general misuse of the model that may go unnoticed, and should be monitored carefully, lies in the fact that the personal approach to risk of top management may not conform with the approach to risk of the main stakeholders. Confusing the two may lead to top management planning that does not adhere to the unwritten objectives of the main stakeholders.

Variations, additions

Even though return is a non-composite variable, it takes into account the following:

- Market research data,

- Management's subjective trade-offs between risk and return.

These may be estimated by one of several methods: utility estimation procedures[4] or analysis based on conjoint analysis approaches.[5]

A corporate utility function may be added to the risk–return graph in order to calculate the optimal position on the efficiency frontier, subject to the corporate risk–return trade-off.[6] One must note that corporate (stakeholders') utility may not be identical to senior managers' utilities, and take care not to confuse them in this type of analysis.

In this book we examine risk and return at two levels only: SBU and corporate. The risk–return approach can be applied at any level of the corporate hierarchy. In fact, Cardozo and Wind discuss the approach at the SBU and product-line levels. They break the SBU down into product lines or investments, calculating the average return for each investment. Return for the SBU is then the average of average returns on individual investments, weighted by the resources allocated to each investment.

Thus the model can assist management at the basic business level, with regard to which product lines should be added or dropped. Cardozo and Wind consider it unique in its handling of new product development, as the environmental analysis of future scenarios may indicate opportunities for new product–market groups. New products can be placed on the risk–return graph along with existing products to assess where they are forecasted to appear in relationship to the efficient frontier of the product lines of the SBU at hand. Productivity at the business level is computed by the weighted expected average return and risk of all the investments in the reference SBU.

Derkinderen and Crum[7] have also stressed the importance of assessing returns with risk in their PARE (Potential And Resilience Evaluation) model. Their model has composite axes: potential is measured by opportunities and the action range available to the reference firm, and resilience is measured by the risk the reference firm can handle and its endurance.

Braurs,[8] in his essay-survey of risk and return, uses the same concept of return and variance of return in an efficiency frontier approach. The main difference is that Braurs considers covariance an important issue worth measuring, since negative direct covariance in a portfolio can lead to higher returns than the sum of the individual investments. This could well be the financial basis for calculating synergism or the return on synergism, although no author has yet formalized this concept.

Braurs[8] quotes from Hertz and Thomas[9] a long list of other uses and applications for risk analysis (other than project analysis), that include items useful for business portfolio strategies. Among these are acquisition of another existing firm, closing down a plant, securities in a bank or other financial service company such as an insurance firm, and many other decisions at the business level: storage decisions, short-/long-term marketing decisions, and so on. The reader seeking ideas specific to his/her industry should refer to this application-rich reference.

Cardozo and Wind note that when facilities are shared by businesses, some corporations allocate costs among them, others combine returns, and still others make no attempt to allocate them. Cardozo and Wind adopt the SBU approach in which the joint facilities have already been allocated, so that SBUs are defined separately and independently.

Custom-made portfolio

9

Now that you have been exposed to seven different matrix portfolio approaches, you may feel that none of them exactly applies to your corporation. For example, you may feel that your corporation's planning focus is different from those guiding the existing models; or that the 'reality' expressed by the assumptions behind each approach does not reflect the culture or political system in your corporation or in the countries in which you operate. You or your staff may want to build a matrix catering to the specific conditions in which your corporation operates.

Your private model

Wind and Mahajan[1] as well as Hussey[2] point out that many corporations use custom-made matrix portfolio approaches designed to embed their particular world view and specific needs. You may do the same.

The size of the corporation, number of SBUs and their relative sizes, the nature of the industries and markets, the historical development of the corporation, external constraints on its operations, and public interests, are a few of the factors that may create special planning needs and a unique reality.

One way to fulfil these needs is by iterative use of the existing models, a topic discussed in the next chapter. In this chapter we focus on creating a custom-made matrix.

Modifying an existing matrix vs. devising a new matrix

There are two basic ways to create your matrix:

1. Choosing an existing matrix portfolio grid and modifying it to fit your special needs.

2. Starting from scratch.

If one of the existing grids basically suits your corporation you may use it as a basis for modification. However, if you conceive of your custom-made matrix as a synthesis of two or more grids, you may start with one of the grids (the most suitable one, of course) and modify it according to other grids.

Starting from scratch and making modifications each involves several decisions, including definition of axes, grid, cells, variables, graphical presentation, and preferred configuration of the planned portfolio.

Your discretion

Grinding the axes

You may define the X and Y axes according to your needs, but we still recommend you use the convention whereby the X axis relates to the relative competitive position of each SBU, and the Y axis relates to the industry or target market. The Z axis may also be used to portray one variable of your choice.

Cutting the grid

You may choose any of the grids used by existing approaches:

1. 2×2

2. 3×3

3. 5×3

4. 4×5

Alternatively, you can define your own grid. However, we strongly believe a finer division than a 5×5 grid is not required. Remember, you'll have to name each cell. If you face difficulties in distinguishing between neighboring cells, perhaps you don't need so refined a subdivision. On the other hand, if you find some of your cells are too crowded with meanings and different kinds of SBUs and strategies, you should consider a higher-level grid.

Naming the cells

Though it may seem a boring and thankless chore, and even slightly childish, to name cells and call them 'Leader', 'Frog' or 'Double or Quit', we strongly urge you to be very meticulous in naming the cells in your new grid. Corporations, especially at the higher echelons, tend to think in metaphors. Dealing in detail with up to a hundred SBUs, and sometimes more, can be very fatiguing. Thus, higher-level executives tend to define some SBUs as 'the core of our business', some as 'cashables', and the like. The introduction of the matrix portfolio in the late 1960s, and its widespread use in the 1970s and 1980s, made the 'Milking Cow' and 'Problem Child' corporate household terms.

Use of accepted terms, either taken from existing approaches presented in this book, or original names which capture your corporation's culture and strategy, will enhance your custom-made matrix, as well as communications among top-level executives.

Choosing the variables

To use the custom-made model, values for the variables you choose should be assigned. Every variable discussed in this book is at your disposal, but you may define new variables, which you may term according to your needs. Your X and Y axes may be single-dimensional (by assigning one variable to each) or multifactor (by assigning a number of variables to one or both axes). However, should you decide to use the third, Z axis, we recommend you use a single-dimensional axis. Any variable may be assigned to this axis, as well as to the other two. Remember, it is your responsibility.

We strongly believe that about 10 variables, per axis, are more than enough; try not to overdo it.

Filling the bubbles

Throughout, we use the bubbles to graphically present total sales in the relevant industry/market, while the colored wedge indicates our market share in this market. However, as you probably remember, some of the approaches employ different practices. For example, the original BCG model uses the bubble to represent the *SBU's* sales or assets. We welcome you to use the bubbles for these variables or any other *single* variable, including one already included in one of the axes.

Configuring the future

Your optimal portfolio is a product of your corporation goals. You may prefer an inventory of start-ups, heavy short-term cash flow, or any feasible combination. The guidelines for portfolio planning should be spelled out very clearly. Once the graphical presentation of your existing portfolio is finished, planning, both graphical and numerical, should follow its guidelines.

10

Summary and conclusions

Summary

Using matrix analysis as the base point, seven different corporate portfolio models have been presented in this book, to enable the complete representation of the corporate mix of business units which guides strategy making at the corporate level. You have been able to study the different models, learn how to use each of them and how to benefit from the multi-model approach to corporate strategy analysis.

You will be able to systematically break down your corporate strategy into identifiable components and subsequently reconstruct a recognizable comprehensive strategic profile. Having constructed your strategic profile, you will be able to:

1. Identify your corporate strategy,

2. Search for strategic alternatives,

3. Highlight normative prescriptions by various portfolio models, and

4.   Make 'What if' analyses.

To help you recall what you have learned while reading this book, we will summarize the different portfolio models and the ways in which they can be used in analyzing your corporate strategy.

Strategy is created at the topmost level of the organization. This level, either intentionally or not, sets the organization's goals and decides on its investments and the deployment of resources. Although many other forces have their impact, it is the mandate of top management to make strategy. In this book, we have divided strategy into:

1.   Corporate strategy (covering many business units),

2.   Business-level strategy (for one business unit),

3.   Functional strategy (such as finance, information systems, or marketing).

The highest level of strategy making of single business unit organizations is the business level. However, for the many large organizations that are corporations, composed of multi-industry or multi-product–market units, corporate strategy is the highest level. This book focuses on the corporate level, allowing you to analyze the group of different strategic business units comprising the corporation.

A multi-model approach to corporate portfolio analysis

In this book we present a multi-model approach to corporate portfolio analysis which offers you the benefits of all the important approaches without subjecting you to the limitations inherent in using a single approach. It is an attempt to answer the need for a universal framework for corporate portfolio analysis.

In Chapters 2–8, seven different corporate portfolio models are presented and discussed. While each one of the models is well known and has its own following, they all have their limitations and have received their share of criticism. By using the different approaches interactively, a new and better tool for corporate strategy making is presented in this book.

The concept of the corporate portfolio

Relating as it does to a complex set of business units which may be quite different from each other in nature, corporate strategy is very different from business strategy. Classification or categorization tools (graphical if possible) are required to identify, present, and describe the business unit mix.

In order to analyze your corporate portfolio and current mix of business units (which together make up the corporate portfolio), you are asked in this book to evaluate and collect data on the corporation's various business units. Subsequently you can use the data to analyze your corporate portfolio according to different portfolio models.

Common to all models of portfolio planning is the unit of analysis – the strategic business unit (SBU). The first step of accurately designating the SBUs is crucial to the quality of the portfolio analysis. Chapter 1 constitutes a comprehensive guide to the process of defining the corporation's various SBUs.

Implicit in the identification of the SBU is the definition of its market/industry. The delineation of the SBU's boundaries is to a large degree derived from the market it serves and the industry to which it belongs.

Once all the SBUs have been defined, the various portfolio approaches can be used to analyze corporate strategy. Each portfolio approach has a planning focus, which is the pattern that emerges from the completed matrix on which all the corporation's SBUs appear. Examples of planning focus are: cash flow, return on investment, risk–return ratio and life-cycle stage distribution. While some portfolio approaches maintain a single planning focus, others are based upon a combination of goal functions.

The typical portfolio matrix is two-dimensional, the two axes being the basic strategic characteristics according to which the different business units are positioned within the matrix. One dimension usually represents external characteristics (market or industry), the other internal factors (competence or competitive position). The intersection of the paired values on the two axes relating to a given SBU determines its location within the portfolio matrix. The total portfolio area is subdivided into cells.

Each portfolio model is based on a number of strategic variables, which are usually classified into six groups of metavariables: strategy, strategy making, structure, environment, performance and basic characteristics. In each chapter, the strategic variables relevant to the portfolio model under discussion are listed. Full definitions are provided the first time the variable is encountered. The various models discussed in this book are summarized below.

The BCG portfolio matrix

The Boston Consulting Group (BCG) portfolio model is a four-cell matrix which focuses on cash flow. The external/vertical axis represents market growth rate, and the internal/horizontal axis represents the SBU's relative competitive strength, measured by its relative market share.

The SBUs are plotted as circles on the two-dimensional layout, each circle in the two-by-two grid representing an SBU. The relative size of the business unit is represented by the shaded pie wedge of the circle, the size of the circle being proportional to the total size of the market.

The BCG matrix assigns a generic name to all SBUs located within each of the four areas of the grid as follows:

Star   high market growth rate/high relative market share,

Cash Cow   low market growth rate/high relative market share,

Question Mark   high market growth rate/low relative market share,

Dog   low market growth rate/low relative market share.

The matrix is balanced when the Cash Cow SBUs have enough cash to support the Question Mark SBUs, as well as some of the Stars, which in time will become Cash Cows themselves.

The main limitation of this growth-share matrix is that by itself it is not very useful for determining strategy for a particular business. To determine operational strategies, other models must be utilized in addition to the BCG model. The BCG model is no substitute for business-level strategy making, and it does not dictate strategy. It is merely a description (or presentation) of the current situation or future prospects as evaluated on the basis of certain available data. The BCG matrix is best applied to portfolios whose SBUs make items in large quantities, and compete strongly in simple, unsophisticated markets based on strict price competition.

The GE/McKinsey portfolio matrix

The GE/McKinsey matrix is a multifactor portfolio approach to strategic planning. It is a two-dimensional, nine-cell matrix which focuses on future profits. SBUs are rated as candidates for future investment in terms of both quantifiable and qualitative elements. The X and Y axes of the GE/McKinsey matrix represent overall measures of business strength (or competitive position) and industry (or product–market) attractiveness, respectively. Each axis represents a composite of multiple quantitative and qualitative factors.

SBUs are plotted as circles on the two-dimensional, three-by-three grid. The market share of an SBU within its industry is represented by a pie wedge of the circle, which represents total sales of the industry.

The nine-cell matrix is divided into three areas: green, yellow and red. Firms falling in the green area are considered Winners, those falling in the yellow area are Profit Producers, Average Businesses or Question Marks, and those situated in the red area are Losers. The GE/McKinsey matrix proposes generic strategies for each area, as well as more specific strategies for SBUs situated in the individual cells.

This matrix should be used to display both the present position of the corporation's SBUs and their future position. In general, the strategy offered by the model will be to increase resources to SBUs with high industry attractiveness and strong competitive position. Conversely, SBUs with low industry attractiveness and a weak competitive position will have their resource allocations reduced.

The main focus of the GE/McKinsey matrix is the balancing of investments, and the matrix should be used for this purpose. Another use is competitor analysis. A competitor's portfolio may be assessed at different points in time, to help gain insight into its corporate strategies and policies.

The DPM/Shell portfolio matrix

The DPM/Shell portfolio matrix was originally developed for a capital-intensive oil corporation. It is a two-dimensional, three-by-three matrix based on multiple measures, deriving from variables which are both quantitative and qualitative. Compared to the GE/McKinsey model, the original DPM/Shell model is more quantitative, more precise in factor-rating assessment, and has more explicit generic strategies. It considers both cash flow and ROI and it takes the different stages of the life cycle into account.

The X axis, labeled 'competitive capability', represents the competence of the SBU or its ability to take advantage of opportunities in the sector in which it is located. The Y axis, labeled 'business sector prospects', represents the attractiveness of the sector in which the SBU is operating.

Each cell in the DPM/Shell matrix has its own explicit strategy, as described in detail in Chapter 4. The cells are termed: Leader, Growth, Cash Generator, Try Harder, Proceed with Care or Custodial, Phased Withdrawal, Double or Quit, Phased Withdrawal/Proceed with Care, Divest.

This model is particularly effective for visualizing development and change over time, since it does not rely on financial or historical data. Thus, it can be used to evaluate portfolios even at the planning stage.

Although the DPM/Shell matrix aspires to be more objective and precise in its approach than the GE/McKinsey model, it still allows for much subjectivity in management's choice of measures.

The Hofer–Schendel product–market evolution portfolio matrix

The product–market evolution portfolio matrix was developed explicitly to analyze new businesses in new markets, that is, businesses that are just beginning to grow. The model concentrates on positioning existing SBUs in the product–market evolution matrix, establishing an ideal future portfolio on the matrix, and identifying strategies for achieving this ideal portfolio, which can be done either by acquiring or selling SBUs and/or by changing or enhancing the strategies of current SBUs.

The position of each SBU is defined according to the maturity of its market and its strength relative to the competition. Different business-level strategies can be set according to the life-cycle stage of the SBU's product–market. At the corporate level, three types of ideal portfolios are offered by the model: a growth portfolio, a profit portfolio, and a balanced portfolio.

The X and Y axes represent relative competitive position and product–market stage evolution, respectively. The X axis is divided into three sections, the Y axis into five, creating a three-by-five grid. The position of the SBU within the matrix indicates the recommended generic strategy. The model proposes six generic strategies, which are discussed in detail in Chapter 5: share-increasing, growth, profit, market concentration and asset reduction, turnaround, liquidation and divestiture.

The Hofer–Schendel model may be usefully applied to balancing the corporate portfolio and assigning business strategies to each SBU. It can be used to establish the desired corporate portfolio profile, to formulate specific business strategies for each SBU, and to close any gap existing between corporate and SBU-level strategies. The model can also be used for competitor analysis at the corporate and SBU level.

The ADL life-cycle portfolio matrix

The ADL life-cycle portfolio matrix is based on the assumption that an SBU is situated in one of four life-cycle stages – embryonic, growth, maturity or aging – and should be analyzed accordingly. In addition to the life-cycle stage, the competitive position of the SBU relative to other SBUs competing in the same industry is defined. The SBU is classified as holding one of five basic competitive positions: dominant, strong, favorable, tenable, weak. Each SBU is analyzed separately to determine the development stage of its industry, and its competitive position within this industry. The combination of these two multifactor dimensions – four industry life-cycle stages and five competitive positions – constitutes the ADL's 20-cell matrix.

ADL proposes a very elaborate set of strategic planning options for the business level, based on the position of the SBU in the matrix.

Strategy planning is performed in three consecutive steps. First the 'natural thrust' of the SBU is determined on the basis of its position in the matrix. Within each natural thrust, SBUs may have different 'specific thrusts', which still constitute a general strategic guideline. Subsequently, a generic strategy is chosen, which includes operational planning (a comprehensive discussion of the different thrusts and the generic strategies can be found in Chapter 6.

The basic concept of the ADL model is that the corporate's portfolio should be balanced, meaning that SBUs should be distributed throughout the life-cycle stages, cash flow should be positive, and average weighted RONA (return on net assets) should meet corporate goals.

In addition to presenting the competitive position and life-cycle stage of the SBU, ADL uses the matrix format in order to exhibit the financial contribution of the SBUs on the grid to the corporate portfolio. The matrix is used to display the distribution of sales, net income assets and RONA by life-cycle stage and competitive positioning. The ADL approach assumes that most industries follow the life-cycle pattern in the prescribed order, though the length of the cycle may vary from industry to industry.

This model is particularly useful for high-tech industries in which life cycles are very short and for which, if the proper strategies are not taken at the proper time, an SBU can fall short of its goals.

Hussey's risk portfolio matrix

One of the underlying concepts of the portfolio approach is that risk may be spread to ensure a certain stability of sales and profits. It is often pointed out that risk is just as fundamental a consideration of a given investment as are projected profits. Hussey's risk portfolio matrix is in fact a three-dimensional extension of the DPM matrix, the X axis being the SBU competitive position, the Y axis representing its market sector's profitability, and the Z axis, the third dimension, depicting risk.

The nine cells created by the X and Y axes are almost identical to those of the DPM matrix. They are: Leader, Try Harder, Double or Quit, Growth, Proceed with Care, Cash Generator, Phased Withdrawal which appears twice, and Divestment. Each SBU is scored on three factors and positioned on the grid accordingly. Thus, risk, defined as any factor or event in the environment that may have an adverse effect on the SBU, is assessed for each SBU, simultaneously with its competitive position and market sector probability. Hussey's risk matrix is utilized to assess the significant external influences on a particular business, and the consequences of adverse effects on the product portfolio, as well as the probability of these adverse effects actually occurring.

The objective of the risk matrix is to create and maintain a portfolio of businesses that earn an acceptable rate of return in accordance with the level of risk they incur. At the corporate level, risk is spread across the portfolio. At the SBU level, the model focuses upon the attainment of a return which is commensurate with the inherent level of risk. The acceptable ratios of risk and return are dictated by stakeholders.

The risk matrix is used to explore and examine key environmental factors and their potential influence upon individual SBUs and the corporate portfolio as a whole. The approach enables management to include these factors in the strategic decision-making process and to anticipate the possible outcomes of a chosen strategy. The risk matrix can be utilized to generate scenarios of risk relating to competitor behavior. However, such an analysis is difficult, as estimating the impact of adverse changes on a competitor requires intimate knowledge of its position and strategy.

The Cardozo–Wind risk–return portfolio matrix

The Cardozo–Wind risk–return portfolio matrix aims to increase the productivity of SBU investments. The model has risk on the X axis and return on the Y axis as the basic criteria for mapping and evaluating the business portfolio. Its main use is to evaluate the productivity of a current portfolio of businesses, to assess future scenarios, and finally to evaluate possible additions to and removals from the portfolio.

The basic premise of the model is that whereas all managers strive to maximize the productivity of their portfolios of SBUs, each has his/her personal approach to risk. The principle of the model is that for every degree of risk an SBU manager takes, there is a specific level of expected return. The most productive set of businesses that the corporation is involved with at a particular time forms an 'efficient frontier' (EF). The EF is a useful benchmark for deciding on adding new businesses via mergers, acquisitions and internal development, or dropping unsuccessful businesses. Another useful criterion is the hurdle rate – a specific level of expected return designated as the minimum requirement for management to embark on a particular investment.

After calculating the individual expected return and risk characteristics, the SBUs are plotted on a two-dimensional risk–return graph. Both the EF and the hurdle rate are drawn on the graph as well. SBUs that fall under a specific return rate are automatically rejected. Subsequently the graph is divided into four areas, and each area described in terms of risk and return.

The Cardozo–Wind model enables managers to analyze new and potential SBUs. The manager deals explicitly with the future, and evaluates possible strategies by projecting future outcomes. The model is a guide for mergers and acquisitions, investments in and divestments of SBUs.

The custom-made portfolio matrix

The custom-made portfolio matrix is your own personal model. You can either start from scratch and create a model that suits your corporation, or you can begin by taking one of the seven grids presented above and adapting it to your needs. You may define your grid, axes, cells, variables, graphical presentation, and preferred configuration of the planned portfolio.

The contribution of this book

Throughout this book you have been learning how to employ the different portfolio matrices presented. We have also tried to show you that different portfolio matrices can be used for various purposes.

Choose a portfolio model

The models presented in this book are based on different assumptions, different goal functions, and different dimensions. Any one of them may be usefully applied in examining corporate strategy. We recommend managers choose one or more portfolio models as a basis for analyzing their corporations.

Identify corporate strategy

By using the variety of portfolio models discussed here, managers can deepen their understanding of current corporate strategy.

Seek strategic alternatives

Theoretically, the multitude of business units within a corporation allows for endless combinations and permutations. In practice, most of these alternative mixes are not viable. On the basis of the normative prescriptions offered by the various models, this book enables managers to focus on a manageable number of possible strategic alternative mixes of SBUs, each of these combinations being consistent with corporate strategy.

Fine-tune strategy with 'what if'

When seeking different points of view, and analyzing different possible future scenarios, managers can use the various models in introducing changes to re-evaluate and fine-tune the alternatives.

This volume is not a textbook on strategy and policy. However, if you have read to this point, you now know a lot about the practicalities of corporate-level strategies and something about business-level strategies. You have been introduced to the main concepts and variables, the important schools of thought, the theories, and the findings. But the most important thing this book teaches you is how to use this knowledge systematically. You have learned how to:

1.   Identify past and current corporate strategies;

2.   Analyze the potentials and limitations of the corporation and its SBUs relative to its competitors;

3. Recognize imbalances in the portfolio;

4. Identify areas for development, acquisition and divestment;

5. Formulate a preferred corporate strategy;

6. Plan to implement the preferred strategy over time.

The approach presented here is comprehensive and integrative, allowing you to deal with seven different portfolio models in detail.

Limitations of this book

We scarcely use financial information. Just as Alice, before going down into Wonderland, doubted the value of books without dialogue or pictures, a manager may doubt the value of a book on strategy that does not consider financial data. To some readers, our use of qualitative rather than quantitative data may seem a little vague and imprecise. Well, that is the way strategies are made. At the beginning of every elaborate and detailed five-year plan, complete with *pro forma* yearly balance sheets and income statements, there is a subjective strategy for the next ten years. Since we focus on corporate strategy making, the result is strategy rather than detailed five-year *pro forma* financial statements.

We relate to some important aspects of business unit strategies, as well as some functional strategies, but we do not elaborate. This book is intended for managers involved in corporate-level strategy making. It takes the CEO's point of view. Those CEOs who also assume responsibility for specific functional strategy making in areas such as finance, marketing, production, R&D, manpower, or information systems, will find it insufficient for their needs in the functional area and are advised to complement it with books that focus on the strategies of the specific functional areas.

This book does not deal with particular business-level strategy typologies. If you are interested in learning more about business-level strategy you might read *Business SUCCESS,* by Eli Segev and Paul Gray.

Most importantly, remember that we present a diagnostic tool at the manager's disposal. It provides direction but not direct solutions. Do not expect analysis to dictate which specific SBU a corporation should target for development or acquisition. By using the various models, managers will learn to recognize when the corporate portfolio is imbalanced. Furthermore, they will be able to discern the qualities desirable in a candidate for acquisition or development to rectify the imbalance. Should the manager have a specific SBU in mind, any or all of the models may be used to check the fit of the SBU to the needs of the portfolio and to corporate strategy.

Conclusion: Applying portfolio models to your corporation

The seven portfolio models presented here offer a rich set of alternatives. They allow you to view your portfolio through different eyes. The models are tools that help you in long-range planning for your corporation. Each portfolio model has a different view of the world because it is based on different assumptions and emphasizes different aspects of strategy.

Having understood the various portfolio models, the natural question is how to apply them to your corporation. The first step is to sharpen your mental model of your corporation and your own approach to the world. You may want to begin with focus. Are you worried about survival? Performance? The way you make strategy? Next you may want to consider which SBUs are critical to your corporation. You may also ask yourself if you are comfortable with the basic assumptions of the models. Do they conform to your world outlook? Which combination of strategic variables is important to your corporation? Are you concerned with corporate cash flow or profit levels or risk or a combination of these planning goals? Is mark/industry attractiveness or the life-cycle stage the most appropriate dimension of analysis for your corporate portfolio? Are you more interested in assessing your present situation or in planning for the future?

Once you have constructed your mental model, you are ready to compare it with the models presented in this book. Remember, the creators of the portfolio models did not tailor the models specifically to your corporation. Thus you cannot expect that one of the models will match your situation exactly. More likely, you will find that several of them come close to emphasizing some of your concerns. If this is the case, we recommend that you evaluate your corporation in terms of these models.

Each model will provide you with different insights about your corporation and each will lead you to new ideas about your corporate strategy. You should, however, synthesize these ideas and insights into a unique strategy for your firm. Be innovative and creative. Do not follow the model and its prescriptions in a mechanical way. Adjust it to your corporation and your situation. Having done this, you are ready to explore the changes you need to make in your corporation to achieve your new strategy.

References

Chapter 1

1.   Chandler, A.D. (1962). *Strategy and Structure*. Cambridge: MIT Press, p. 13.

2.   Hofer, C.W., (1975). 'Toward a contingency theory of business strategy,' *Academy of Management Journal*, Vol. 18, No.4, p.784.

3.   Bourgeois, L.J., III (1980). 'Strategy and environment: a conceptual integration,' *Academy of Management Review*, Vol. 5, No. 1, pp. 25–39.

4.   Goold, Michael and Luchs, Kathleen (1993). 'Why diversify? Four decades of management thinking,' *Academy of Management Executive*, Vol. 7, No. 3, pp. 6–25.

5.   Rue, L. and Holland, P. (1986). *Strategic Management*. New York: McGraw-Hill, pp. 238–40.

6.   Sharpe, William F. (1985). *Investments*. Englewood Cliffs, NJ: Prentice-Hall, p. 140.

'7.   Johnson, Gerry and Scholes, Kevan (1993). *Exploring Corporate Strategy: Text and Cases* (third edition). New York: Prentice-Hall, p. 144.

8.   Wensley, Robin (1981). 'Strategic marketing: Betas, boxes and basics,' *Journal of Marketing*, Vol. 45 (Summer), pp. 173–82.

9.   Wensley, Robin (1982). 'PIMS and BCG: New horizons or false dawn?' *Strategic Management Journal*, Vol. 3 (January-March), pp. 147–58.

10.   Ansoff, Igor H. and McDonnell, Edward J. (1990). *Implanting Strategic Management* (second edition). Englewood Cliffs, NJ: Prentice-Hall.

11.   Day, George S. (1984). *Strategic Market Planning: The Pursuit of Competitive Advantage*. St. Paul, MN: West Publishing Company.

12.   Rowe, Alan J., Mason, Richard O. and Dickel, Karl E. (1982). *Strategic Management and Business Policy: A Methodological Approach*. Reading, MA: Addison-Wesley.

13.   Anderson, C.R. and Paine, F.T. (1975). Managerial Perceptions and Strategic Behavior. *Academy of Management Journal*, Vol. 18, No. 4, pp. 811–23.

14.   Arthur D. Little, Inc. (1980). *A Management System for the 1980's*. San Francisco, CA.

15.   Day, George S. (1986). *Analysis for Strategic Marketing Decisions*. St. Paul, MN: West Publishing Company.

16.   Hofer, C.W. and Schendel, D, (1978). *Strategy Formulation: Analytical Concepts*. St. Paul, MN: West Publishing Company.

17.   Harvey, Donald F. (1982). *Business Policy and Strategic Management*. Columbus OH: Charles Merril Publishing.

18.   Rowe, Alan J., Mason, Richard O. and Dickel, Karl E. (1982). *Strategic Management and Business Policy: A Methodological Approach*. Reading, MA: Addison-Wesley, p. 167.

19.   Abell, Derek F. and Hammond, John S. (1979). *Strategic Market Planning: Problems and Analytical Approaches*. Englewood Cliffs, NJ: Prentice-Hall.

20.   Day, George S. (1981). 'Strategic market analysis and definition: An integrated approach,' *Strategic Management Journal*, Vol. 2 (July–September) pp. 281–99.

21.   Day, George S. (1981). 'Strategic Market Analysis and Definition: An Integrated Approach,' *Strategic Management Journal*, Vol. 2 (July–September) pp. 281–99.

22.   Porter, M.E., (1980). *Competitive Strategy: Techniques for Analysing Industries and Competitors*. New York: Free Press.

23.   Hussey, David E. (1978). 'Portfolio analysis: Practical experience with the directional policy matrix,' *Long Range Planning*, Vol. 11 (August), pp. 2–8.

24.   Andrews, K.R. (1971). *The Concept of Corporate Strategy*. Homewood, IL: Dow Jones-Irwin.

25.   Boston Consulting Group Staff (1968, reprinted 1970, 1972). *Perspectives on Experience*. Boston: Boston Consulting Group.

26.   Chandler, A.D. (1962). *Strategy and Structure*. Cambridge: MIT Press.

27.   Glueck, W.F. (1976). *Business Policy: Strategy Formation and Management Action*. New York: McGraw-Hill.

28.   Rumelt, R.P. (1974). *Strategy and Economic Performance*. Boston: Harvard University Press.

29.   Aharoni, Y. (1966). *The Foreign Investment Decisions Process*. Boston: Division of Research, Graduate School of Business Administration, Harvard University.

30.   Allison, G.T. (1971). *Essence of Decision: Explaining the Cuban Missile Crisis*. Boston: Little, Brown.

31.   Ansoff, H.I. (1965). *Corporate Strategy*. New York: McGraw-Hill.

32.   Bower, J. (1970). *Managing the Resource Allocation Process*. Boston: Division of Research, Graduate School of Business Administration, Harvard University.

33.   Cyert, R.M. and March, J.G. (1963). *A Behavioral Theory of the Firm*. Englewood Cliffs, NJ: Prentice-Hall.

34.   Mintzberg, H. (1973). 'Strategy making in three modes,' *California Management Review*, Vol. 16, No. 2, pp. 44–53.

35.   Chandler, A.D., (1962). *Strategy and Structure*. Cambridge: MIT Press, p.13.

36.   Channon, D.F. (1973). *The Strategy and Structure of British Enterprise*. Boston: Division of Research, Graduate School of Business Administration, Harvard University.

37.   Child, J. (1972). 'Organizational structure, environment, and performance: the role of strategic choice,' *Sociology*, Vol. 6, pp. 1–22.

38.   Galbraith, J.R. and Nathanson, D.A. (1978). *Strategy Implementation: Role of Structure and Process*. St. Paul, MN: West Publishing Company.

39.   Lawrence, P. and Lorsch, J. (1967). *Organization and Environment*, Boston: Division of Research, Graduate School of Business Administration, Harvard University.

40.   Perrow, C. (1970). *Organizational Analysis: A Sociological View*. Monterey, CA: Brooks/Cole.

41.   Woodward, J. (1965). *Industrial Organization*. London: Oxford University Press.

42.   Anderson, C.R. and Paine, F.T. (1975). 'Managerial perceptions and strategic behavior,' *Academy of Management Journal*, Vol. 18, No. 4, pp. 811–23.

43.   Duncan, R.B. (1972). 'Characteristics of organizational environments and perceived environmental uncertainty,' *Administrative Science Quarterly*, Vol. 18, No. 2, pp. 313–27.

44.   Emery, F.E. and Trist E.L. (1965). 'The casual texture of organizational environments,' *Human Relations*, Vol. 18, pp. 21–32.

45.   Lawrence, P. and Lorsch, J. (1967). *Organization and Environment*. Boston: Division of Research, Graduate School of Business Administration, Harvard University.

46.   Johnson, Gerry and Scholes, Kevan (1993). *Exploring Corporate Strategy: Text and Cases* (third edition). New York: Prentice-Hall, p. 106.

47.·   Haspeslagh, Philippe (1982). 'Portfolio planning: Uses and limits,' *Harvard Business Review,* Vol. 60 (January-February), pp. 58–73.

Chapter 2

1.   Boston Consulting Group Staff (1968, reprinted 1970, 1972). *Perspectives on Experience*. Boston: Boston Consulting Group.

2.   Johnson, Gerry and Scholes, Kevan (1993). *Exploring Corporate Strategy: Text and Cases* (third edition). New York: Prentice-Hall.

3.   Levitt, Theodore (1965). 'Exploit the life cycle,' *Harvard Business Review*, Vol. 43 (November-December), pp. 81–94.

4.   Glueck, William F. and Jauch, Lawrence R. (1984). *Business Policy and Strategic Management*. New York: McGraw-Hill Book Company.

5.   Rowe, Alan J., Mason, Richard O. and Dickel, Karl E. (1982). *Strategic Management and Business Policy: A Methodological Approach*. Reading, MA: Addison-Wesley.

6.   Day, George S. (1977). 'Diagnosing the product portfolio,' *Journal of Marketing*, Vol. 41 (April), pp. 29–38.

7.   *Forbes*, October 15, 1977, Vol. 120, p. 132.

8.   Weiss, Fred and Tallett, Elizabeth (1986). 'Corporate portfolio analysis,' in Gardner and Rachlins (eds.), *Handbook of Strategic Planning*. New York: John Wiley.

9.   *Business Week* (1983, June 27). 'The future catches up with a strategic planner,' p. 62.

10.   Ansoff, Igor H. and McDonnell, Edward J. (1990). *Implanting Strategic Management* (second edition). Englewood Cliffs, NJ: Prentice-Hall.

11.   Stahl, Michael J. and Grigsby, David W. (1992). *Strategic Management for Decision Making*. Boston, MA: PWS-Kent Publishing Company.

12.   David, Fred R. (1991). *Concepts of Strategic Management* (third edition). New York: Macmillan, pp. 221–24.

13.   Day, George S. (1986). *Analysis for Strategic Marketing Decisions*. St. Paul, MN: West Publishing Company.

14.   Porter, M.E., (1980). *Competitive Strategy: Techniques for Analysing Industries and Competitors*. New York: Free Press.

15.   Robey, Daniel (1991). *Designing Organizations* (third edition). Homewood, IL: Irwin.

16.   Hax, Arnoldo C. and Majluf, Nicolas S. (1983). 'The use of the growth-share matrix in strategic planning,' *Interfaces*, Vol. 13, No. 1 (February), pp. 46–60.

17.   Rowe, Alan J., Mason, Richard O. and Dickel, Karl E. (1982). *Strategic Management and Business Policy: A Methodological Approach*. Reading, MA: Addison-Wesley.

18.   Sharplin, Arthur (1985). *Strategic Management*. New York: McGraw-Hill Book Company.

19.   Mintzberg, Henry and Quinn, James Brian (1991). *The Strategic Process, Concepts, Contexts, Cases* (second edition). Englewood Cliffs, NJ: Prentice-Hall, pp. 678–80.

20.   Rowe, Alan J., Mason, Richard O. and Dickel, Karl E. (1982). *Strategic Management and Business Policy: A Methodological Approach.* Reading, MA: Addison-Wesley.

21.   Wheelen, Thomas L. and Hunger, David J. (1992). *Strategic Management and Business Policy* (fourth edition). Reading, MA: Addison-Wesley.

22.   Thompson, Arthur A., Jr. and Strickland, A.J., III (1990). *Strategic Management, Concepts and Cases* (fifth edition). Homewood, IL: Irwin, p. 199.

23.   Harvey, Donald F. (1982). *Business Policy and Strategic Management.* Columbus OH: Charles Merril Publishing.

24.   Byars, Lloyd L. (1991). *Strategic Management – Formulation and Implementation – Concepts and Cases* (third edition). New York: HarperCollins.

25.   Hax, Arnoldo C. and Majluf, Nicolas S. (1983). 'The use of the growth-share matrix in strategic planning,' *Interfaces*, Vol. 13, No. 1 (February), pp. 46–60.

26.   Harvey, Donald F. (1982). *Business Policy and Strategic Management.* Columbus OH: Charles Merril Publishing.

27.   Byars, Lloyd L. (1991). *Strategic Management – Formulation and Implementation – Concepts and Cases* (third edition). New York: HarperCollins.

28.   Porter, M.E. (1980). *Competitive Strategy: Techniques for Analysing Industries and Competitors.* New York: Free Press.

29.   Ansoff, Igor H. and McDonnell, Edward J. (1990). *Implanting Strategic Management* (second edition). Englewood Cliffs, NJ: Prentice-Hall.

30.   Buzzell, Robert D., Gale, Bradley T. and Sultan, Ralph G.M. (1975). 'Market share: A key to profitability,' *Harvard Business Review*, Vol. 53 (January–February) pp. 97–107.

31.   *Forbes*, October 15, 1977, Vol. 120, p. 132.

32.   Sharplin, Arthur (1985). *Strategic Management.* New York: McGraw-Hill Book Company.

33.   Byars, Lloyd L. (1991). *Strategic Management – Formulation and Implementation – Concepts and Cases* (third edition). New York: HarperCollins.

34. Rue, L. and Holland, P. (1986). *Strategic Management*. New York: McGraw-Hill.

35. Rowe, Alan J., Mason, Richard O. and Dickel, Karl E. (1982). *Strategic Management and Business Policy: A Methodological Approach*. Reading, MA: Addison-Wesley.

36. Weiss, Fred and Tallett, Elizabeth (1986). 'Corporate portfolio analysis,' in Gardner and Rachlins (eds.), *Handbook of Strategic Planning*. New York: John Wiley.

37. Boston Consulting Group, (1968, reprinted 1970, 1972). *Perspectives on Experience*.

38. Buzzell, Robert D. and Gale, Bradley T. (1987). *The PIMS Principles*. New York: The Free Press.

39. Henderson, Bruce D. (1979). *Henderson on Corporate Strategy*. Cambridge, MA: Abt Books.

40. Harvey, Donald F. (1982). *Business Policy and Strategic Management*. Columbus OH: Charles Merril Publishing.

41. Wensley, Robin (1982). 'PIMS and BCG: New horizons or false dawn?' *Strategic Management Journal*, Vol. 3 (January–March), pp. 147–58.

42. Sharplin, Arthur (1985). *Strategic Management*. New York: McGraw-Hill Book Company.

43. Porter, M.E. (1980). *Competitive Strategy: Techniques for Analysing Industries and Competitors*. New York: Free Press.

44. Rumelt, Richard P. (1979). 'Evaluation of strategy: Theory and models,' in Schendel, Dan E. and Hofer Charles W. (eds.), *Strategic Management*. Boston: Little Brown pp. 196–211

45. Channon, Derek F. (1979). 'Commentary – on Grant and King,' in Schendel D.E. and Hofer, C.W. (eds.), *Strategic Management – A New View of Business Policy and Planning*. Boston: Little, Brown, pp. 122–33.

46. Sharplin, Arthur (1985). *Strategic Management*. New York: McGraw-Hill Book Company.

47. Ansoff, Igor H. and McDonnell, Edward J. (1990). *Implanting Strategic Management* (second edition). Englewood Cliffs, NJ: Prentice-Hall.

48. Wensley, Robin (1982). 'PIMS and BCG: New Horizons or False Dawn?' *Strategic Management Journal*, Vol. 3 (January–March), pp. 147–58.

49.   Day, George S. (1981). 'Strategic market analysis and definition: An integrated approach,' *Strategic Management Journal*, Vol. 2 (July–September), pp. 281–99.

50.   Day, George S. (1977). 'Diagnosing the product portfolio,' *Journal of Marketing*, Vol. 41 (April), pp. 29–38.

51.   Aaker, David A. (1984). *Developing Business Strategies*. New York: John Wiley, p. 184.

52.   Channon, Derek F. (1979). 'Commentary – on Grant and King,' in Schendel D.E. and Hofer, C.W. (eds.), *Strategic Management – A New View of Business Policy and Planning*. Boston: Little, Brown, pp. 122–33.

53.   Howe, W. Stewart (1986). *Corporate Strategy*. London: Macmillan.

54.   Wheelen, Thomas L. and Hunger, David J. (1992). *Strategic Management and Business Policy* (fourth edition). Reading, MA: Addison-Wesley.

55.   Ansoff, Igor H. and McDonnell, Edward J. (1990). *Implanting Strategic Management* (second edition). Englewood Cliffs, NJ: Prentice-Hall.

56.   Buzzell, Robert D. and Gale, Bradley T. (1987). *The PIMS Principles*. New York: The Free Press.

57.   Wheelen, Thomas L. and Hunger, David J. (1992). *Strategic Management and Business Policy* (fourth edition). Reading, MA: Addison-Wesley.

58.   Ansoff, Igor H. and McDonnell, Edward J. (1990). *Implanting Strategic Management* (second edition). Englewood Cliffs, NJ: Prentice-Hall.

59.   Wheelen, Thomas L. and Hunger, David J. (1992). *Strategic Management and Business Policy* (fourth edition). Reading, MA: Addison-Wesley.

60.   Hofer, C.W. and Dan Schendel (1978). *Strategy Formulation: Analytical Concepts*. St. Paul, MN: West Publishing Company, pp. 31–2.

61.   Derkinderen, Frans G.J. and Crum, Roy L. (1984). 'Pitfalls in using portfolio techniques: Assesing risk and potential,' *Long Range planning*, Vol. 19 (April), pp. 129–36.

62.   Wensley, Robin (1982). 'PIMS and BCG: New horizons or false dawn?' *Strategic Management Journal*, Vol. 3 (January–March), pp. 147–58.

63.   Buzzell, Robert D. and Gale, Bradley T. (1987). *The PIMS Principles*. New York: The Free Press, p. 12.

64.   Hayden, Catherine L. (1986). *The Handbook of Strategic Expertise*. New York: Free Press.

65.   Hofer, C.W. (1977). *Conceptual Constructs for Formulating Corporate and Business Strategies*. Boston: Intercollegiate Case Clearing House.

66.   Wensley, Robin (1982). 'PIMS and BCG: New horizons or false dawn?' *Strategic Management Journal*, Vol. 3 (January–March), pp. 147–58.

67.   Abernathy, William J., and Wayne, Kenneth (1974). 'Limits of the learning-curve,' *Harvard Business Review*, Vol. 52 (September–October), pp. 109–19.

68.   Hamermesh, R.G. (1978). 'Strategies for low market share businesses,' *Harvard Business Review*, (May–June), pp. 95–102.

69.   Abell, Derek F. and Hammond, John S. (1979). *Strategic Market Planning: Problems and Analytical Approaches*. Englewood Cliffs, NJ: Prentice-Hall.

70.   Woo, Carolyn Y. and Cooper, Arnold C. (1982). 'The surprising cases for low market share,' *Harvard Business Review*, Vol. 60 (November–December), pp. 106–13.

71.   Porter, M.E. (1980). *Competitive Strategy: Techniques for Analysing Industries and Competitors*. New York: Free Press.

72.   Aaker, David A. (1984). *Developing Business Strategies*. New York: John Wiley.

73.   Buzzell, Robert D. and Gale, Bradley T. (1987). *The PIMS Principles*. New York: The Free Press, p. 71.

74.   Byars, Lloyd L. (1991). *Strategic Management – Formulation and Implementation – Concepts and Cases* (third edition). New York: HarperCollins.

75.   Jauch, Lawrence R. and Glueck, William F. (1988). *Business Policy and Strategic Management* (fifth edition). New York: McGraw-Hill Book Company.

76.   Wheelen, Thomas L. and Hunger, David J. (1992). *Strategic Management and Business Policy* (fourth edition). Reading, MA: Addison-Wesley.

77.   Harvey, Donald F. (1982). *Business Policy and Strategic Management*. Columbus, OH: Charles Merril Publishing.

78.   McCarthy, Daniel J., Minichiello, Robert J. and Curran, Joseph R. (1979). *Business Policy and Strategy: Concepts and Readings*. Homewood, Illinois: Richard D. Irvin, Inc.

79.   Rowe, Alan J., Mason, Richard O. and Dickel, Karl E. (1982). *Strategic Management and Business Policy: A Methodological Approach*. Reading, MA: Addison-Wesley.

80.   Rumelt, Richard P. (1979). 'Evaluation of strategy: Theory and models,' in Schendel, Dan E. and Hofer, Charles W. (eds.), *Strategic Management*. Boston: Little Brown, pp. 196–211.

81.   Wheelen, Thomas L. and Hunger, David J. (1992). *Strategic Management and Business Policy* (fourth edition). Reading, MA: Addison-Wesley.

82.   Hedley, Barry A. (1977). 'Strategy and the business portfolio,' *Long Range Planning*, Vol. 10 (February), pp. 9–15.

83.   Goodstein, Leonard D., Nolan, Timothy M. and Pfeiffer, J. William (1993). *Applied Strategic Planning: A Comprehensive Guide*. New York: McGraw-Hill, p. 242.

84.   Byars, Lloyd L. (1991). *Strategic Management – Formulation and Implementation – Concepts and Cases* (third edition). New York: HarperCollins.

85.   McNamee, Patrick (1984).'Competitive analysis using matrix displays,' *Long Range Planning*, Vol. 17 (June), pp. 98–114.

86.   Henderson, Bruce D. and Zakon, Alan J. (1983). 'The growth-share matrix in corporate growth strategy,' in Kenneth J. Albert (ed.), *The Strategic Management Handbook*. New York: McGraw-Hill.

87.   Hosmer, La Rue T. (1982). *Strategic Management – Text Cases on Business Policy*. Englewood Cliffs, NJ: Prentice-Hall.

88.   Glueck, W.E. (1986). 'Strategy planning in a new key,' *The Mckinsey Quarterly* (Winter), pp. 18–41.

89.   Harvey, Donald F. (1982). *Business Policy and Strategic Management*. Columbus OH: Charles Merril Publishing.

Chapter 3

1.   Haspeslagh, Philippe (1982). 'Portfolio planning: Uses and limits,' *Harvard Business Review*, Vol. 60 (January–February) pp. 58–73.

2.   Ansoff, Igor H. and McDonnell, Edward J. (1990). *Implanting Strategic Management* (second edition). Englewood Cliffs, NJ: Prentice-Hall.

3.   *Business Week* (1975, April 28). 'Special Report: Corporate planning piercing future fog in the executive suite,' pp. 46–54.

4.   Hosmer, La Rue T. (1982). *Strategic Management – Text Cases on Business Policy*. Englewood Cliffs, NJ: Prentice-Hall.

5.   David, Fred R. (1991). *Concepts of Strategic Management* (third edition). New York: Macmillan, p. 225.

6.   Hax, Arnoldo C. and Majluf, Nicolas S. (1983). 'The use of the growth-share matrix in strategic planning,' *Interfaces*, Vol. 13, No. 1 (February), pp. 46–60.

7.   Day, George S. (1986). *Analysis for Strategic Marketing Decisions*. St. Paul, MN: West Publishing Company.

8.   Hax, Arnoldo C. and Majluf, Nicolas S. (1983). 'The use of the growth-share matrix in strategic planning,' *Interfaces*, Vol. 13, No. 1 (February), pp. 46–60.

9.   Hosmer, La Rue T. (1982). *Strategic Management – Text Cases on Business Policy*. Englewood Cliffs, NJ: Prentice-Hall.

10.   Wind, Yoram and Mahajan, Vijay (1981). 'Designing product and business portfolios,' *Harvard Business Review*, Vol. 59 (January–February), pp. 155–65.

11.   Wheelen, Thomas L. and Hunger, David J. (1992). *Strategic Management and Business Policy* (fourth edition). Reading, MA: Addison-Wesley.

12.   Day, George S. (1986). *Analysis for Strategic Marketing Decisions*. St. Paul, MN: West Publishing Company, p. 204.

13.   Hax, Arnoldo C. and Majluf, Nicolas S. (1983). 'The use of the growth-share matrix in strategic planning,' *Interfaces*, Vol. 13, No. 1 (February), pp. 46–60.

14.   Naylor, Thomas H. (1986). *The Corporate Strategy Matrix*. New York: Basic Books, p. 106.

15.   Porter, M.E. (1980). *Competitive Strategy: Techniques for Analysing Industries and Competitors*. New York: Free Press.

16.   Day, George S. (1986). *Analysis for Strategic Marketing Decisions*. St. Paul, MN: West Publishing Company, pp. 194–97.

17.   Glueck, W.E. (1986). 'Strategy planning in a new key,' *The Mckinsey Quarterly* (Winter), pp. 18–41.

18.   Aaker, David A. (1984). *Developing Business Strategies*. New York: John Wiley.

19.   Abell, Derek F. and Hammond, John S. (1979). *Strategic Market Planning: Problems and Analytical Approaches*. Englewood Cliffs, NJ: Prentice-Hall.

20.   Day, George S. (1986). *Analysis for Strategic Marketing Decisions*. St. Paul, MN: West Publishing Company, p. 200.

21.   Byars, Lloyd L. (1991). *Strategic Management – Formulation and Implementation – Concepts and Cases* (third edition). New York: HarperCollins.

22.   Day, George S. (1986). *Analysis for Strategic Marketing Decisions*. St. Paul, MN: West Publishing Company.

23.   Stahl, Michael J. and Grigsby, David W. (1992). *Strategic Management for Decision Making*. Boston, MA: PWS-Kent Publishing Company.

24.   Chang, Y.N. and Campo-Flores, Fileman (1980). *Business Policy and Strategy*: Texts and Cases. Santa Monica, CA: Goodyear Publishing Company, Inc.

25.   Porter, M.E. (1980). *Competitive Strategy: Techniques for Analysing Industries and Competitors*. New York: Free Press.

26.   Hosmer, La Rue T. (1982). *Strategic Management – Text Cases on Business Policy*. Englewood Cliffs, NJ: Prentice-Hall.

27.   Channon, Derek F. (1979). 'Commentary – on Grant and King,' in Schendel, D.E. and Hofer, C.W. (eds.), *Strategic Management – A New View of Business Policy and Planning*. Boston: Little Brown, pp. 122–33.

28.   Glueck, W.E. (1986). 'Strategy planning in a new key,' *The McKinsey Quarterly* (Winter), pp. 18–41.

29.   Porter, M.E. (1980). *Competitive Strategy: Techniques for Analysing Industries and Competitors*. New York: Free Press, Chapter 12.

30.   Aaker, David A. (1984). *Developing Business Strategies*. New York: John Wiley.

31.   Abell, Derek F. and Hammond, John S. (1979). *Strategic Market Planning: Problems and Analytical Approaches*. Englewood Cliffs, NJ: Prentice-Hall.

32.   Day, George S. (1986). *Analysis for Strategic Marketing Decisions*. St. Paul, MN: West Publishing Company, pp. 200–07.

33.   Hax, Arnoldo C. and Majluf, Nicolas S. (1983). 'The use of the growth-share matrix in strategic planning,' *Interfaces*, Vol. 13, No. 1 (February), pp. 46–60.

34.   Wind, Yoram and Mahajan, Vijay (1981). 'Designing product and business portfolios,' *Harvard Business Review*, Vol. 59 (January–February), pp. 155–65.

35.   Wheelen, Thomas L. and Hunger, David J. (1992). *Strategic Management and Business Policy* (fourth edition). Reading, MA: Addison-Wesley.

36.   Haspeslagh, Philippe (1982). 'Portfolio planning: Uses and limits,' *Harvard Business Review*, Vol. 60 (January–February) pp. 58–73.

37.   Wind, Yoram and Mahajan, Vijay (1981). 'Designing product and business portfolios,' *Harvard Business Review*, Vol. 59 (January–February), pp. 155–65.

38.   Wensley, Robin (1981). 'Strategic marketing: Betas, boxes and basics,' *Journal of Marketing*, Vol. 45 (Summer), pp. 173–82.

39.   Grant, John H. and King, William J. (1979). 'Strategy formulation: Analytical and normative models,' in Schendel, D.E. and Hofer, C.W. (eds.) *Strategic Management – A New View of Business Policy and Planning*. Boston: Little, Brown, pp. 104–22.

40.   Buzzell, Robert D. and Gale, Bradley T. (1987). *The PIMS Principles*. New York: The Free Press.

41.   Day, George S. (1986). *Analysis for Strategic Marketing Decisions*. St. Paul, MN: West Publishing Company.

42.   Abell, Derek F. and Hammond, John S. (1979). *Strategic Market Planning: Problems and Analytical Approaches*. Englewood Cliffs, NJ: Prentice-Hall.

43.   Ohmae, Kenichi (1982). *The Mind of the Strategist: Business Planning for Competitive Advantage*. Harmoundsworth: Penguin Books.

44.   Hichens, R.E., Robinson, S.J.Q., and Wade, D.P. (1978). 'The directional policy matrix: tool for strategic planning,' *Long Range Planning*, Vol. 11 (June), pp. 8–15.

45.   Monieson, D.D. (1978). 'An overview of marketing planning,' *Executive Bulletin*, Conference Board in Canada.

46.   Steiner, George A. and Miner, John B. (1982). *Management Policy and Strategy*. New York: Macmillan.

47.   Thompson, Arthur A., Jr. and Strickland, A.J., III (1990). *Strategic Management, Concepts and Cases* (fifth edition). Homewood, IL: Irwin, p. 201.

48.   Johnson, Gerry and Scholes, Kevan (1993). *Exploring Corporate Strategy: Text and Cases* (third edition). New York: Prentice-Hall, p. 107.

49.   Hayden, Catherine L. (1986). *The Handbook of Strategic Expertise*. New York: Free Press.

50.   Wind, Yoram, Mahajan, Vijay and Swire, D.J. (1983). 'An empirical comparison of standardized portfolio models,' *Journal of Marketing*, Vol. 47 (Spring), pp. 89–99.

51.   Day, George S. (1986). *Analysis for Strategic Marketing Decisions*. St. Paul, MN: West Publishing Company.

52.   Abell, Derek F. and Hammond, John S. (1979). *Strategic Market Planning: Problems and Analytical Approaches*. Englewood Cliffs, NJ: Prentice-Hall.

53.   Hax, Arnoldo C. and Majluf, Nicolas S. (1983). 'The use of the growth-share matrix in strategic planning,' *Interfaces*, Vol. 13, No. 1 (February), pp. 46–60.

Chapter 4

1.   Naylor, Thomas H. (1986). *The Corporate Strategy Matrix*. New York: Basic Books.

2.   Ansoff, Igor H. and McDonnell, Edward J. (1990). *Implanting Strategic Management* (second edition). Englewood Cliffs, NJ: Prentice-Hall.

3.   Day, George S. (1986). *Analysis for Strategic Marketing Decisions*. St. Paul, MN: West Publishing Company, Chapter 7.

4.   Hichens, R.E., Robinson, S.J.Q., and Wade, D.P. (1978). 'The directional policy matrix: tool for strategic planning,' *Long Range Planning* ,Vol. 11 (June), pp. 8–15.

5.   Day, George S. (1986). *Analysis for Strategic Marketing Decisions*. St. Paul, MN: West Publishing Company.

6.   Hichens, R.E., Robinson, S.J.Q., and Wade, D.P. (1978). 'The directional policy matrix: tool for strategic planning,' *Long Range Planning,* Vol. 11 (June), pp. 8–15.

7.   Hussey, David E. (1978). 'Portfolio analysis: Practical experience with the directional policy matrix,' *Long Range Planning*, Vol. 11 (August), pp. 2–8.

8.   Leontiades, Milton (1982). *Management Policy, Strategy, and Plans*. Boston: Little, Brown.

9.   Harvey, Donald F. (1982). *Business Policy and Strategic Management*. Columbus OH: Charles Merril Publishing.

10.   Porter, M.E. (1980). *Competitive Strategy: Techniques for Analysing Industries and Competitors*. New York: Free Press.

11.   McNamee, Patrick (1984). 'Competitive analysis using matrix displays,' *Long Range Planning*, Vol. 17 (June), pp. 98–114.

12.   Leontiades, Milton (1983). *Policy, Strategy and Implementation: Readings and Cases*. New York: Random House Business Division.

13.   Channon, Derek F. (1979). 'Commentary – on Grant and King,' in Schendel, D.E. and Hofer, C.W. (eds.), *Strategic Management – A New View of Business Policy and Planning*. Boston: Little, Brown, pp. 122–33.

14.   Day, George S. (1986). *Analysis for Strategic Marketing Decisions*. St. Paul, MN: West Publishing Company.

15.   Leontiades, Milton (1982). *Management Policy, Strategy, and Plans*. Boston: Little, Brown.

16.   Channon, Derek F. (1979). 'Commentary – on Grant and King,' in Schendel, D.E. and Hofer, C.W. (eds.), *Strategic Management – A New View of Business Policy and Planning*. Boston: Little Brown, pp. 122–33.

17.   Aaker, David A. (1984). *Developing Business Strategies*. New York: John Wiley.

18.   Hussey, David E. (1978). 'Portfolio analysis: Practical experience with the directional policy matrix,' *Long Range Planning*, Vol. 11 (August), pp. 2–8.

19.   Abell, Derek F. and Hammond, John S. (1979). *Strategic Market Planning: Problems and Analytical Approaches*. Englewood Cliffs, NJ: Prentice-Hall.

20.   Hax, Arnoldo C. and Majluf, Nicolas S. (1984). *Strategic Management: An Integrative Perspective*. Englewood Cliffs, NJ: Prentice-Hall.

21.   Hussey, David E. (1978). 'Portfolio analysis: Practical experience with the directional policy matrix,' *Long Range Planning*, Vol. 11 (August), pp. 2–8.

22.   Day, George S. (1986). *Analysis for Strategic Marketing Decisions*. St. Paul, MN: West Publishing Company.

23.   Wind, Yoram, Mahajan, Vijay and Swire, D.J. (1983). 'An empirical comparison of standardized portfolio models,' *Journal of Marketing*, Vol. 47 (Spring), pp. 89–99.

24.   Hussey, David E. (1978). 'Portfolio analysis: Practical experience with the directional policy matrix,' *Long Range Planning*, Vol. 11 (August), pp. 2–8.

25.   Channon, Derek F. (1979). 'Commentary – on Grant and King,' in Schendel, D.E. and Hofer, C.W. (eds.), *Strategic Management – A New View of Business Policy and Planning*. Boston: Little Brown, pp. 122–33.

26.   Weiss, Fred and Tallett, Elizabeth (1986). 'Corporate portfolio analysis,' in Gardner and Rachlins (eds.), *Handbook of Strategic Planning*. New York: John Wiley, Chapter 5.

27.   Hichens, R.E., Robinson, S.J.Q., and Wade, D.P. (1978). 'The directional policy matrix: tool for strategic planning,' *Long Range Planning*, Vol. 11 (June), pp. 8–15.

28.   McNamee, Patrick (1984). 'Competitive analysis using matrix displays,' *Long Range Planning*, Vol. 17 (June), pp. 98–114.

29.   Hichens, R.E., Robinson, S.J.Q., and Wade, D.P. (1978). 'The directional policy matrix: tool for strategic planning,' *Long Range Planning*, Vol. 11 (June), pp. 8–15.

30.   Wind, Yoram and Mahajan, Vijay (1981). 'Designing product and business portfolios,' *Harvard Business Review*, Vol. 59 (January–February), pp. 155–65.

Chapter 5

1.   Hofer, C.W. (1977). *Conceptual Constructs for Formulating Corporate and Business Strategies*. Boston: Intercollegiate Case Clearing House.

2.   Hofer, C.W. and Schendel, D. (1978). *Strategy Formulation: Analytical Concepts*. St. Paul, MN: West Publishing Company.

3.   Thompson, Arthur A., Jr. and Strickland, A.J., III (1990). *Strategic Management, Concepts and Cases* (fifth edition). Homewood, IL: Irwin, p. 203.

4.   Stahl, Michael J. and Grigsby, David W. (1992). *Strategic Management for Decision Making*. Boston, MA: PWS-Kent Publishing Company.

5.   Johnson, Gerry and Scholes, Kevan (1993). *Exploring Corporate Strategy: Text and Cases* (third edition). New York: Prentice-Hall, p. 145.

6.   Hofer, C.W. and Schendel, D. (1978). *Strategy Formulation: Analytical Concepts*. St. Paul, MN: West Publishing Company, p. 130.

7.   Hofer, C.W. (1977). *Conceptual Constructs for Formulating Corporate and Business Strategies*. Boston: Intercollegiate Case Clearing House, p. 7.

8.   Hofer, C.W. and Schendel, D. (1978). *Strategy Formulation: Analytical Concepts*. St. Paul, MN: West Publishing Company, p. 183.

9.   Hofer, C.W. and Schendel, D. (1978). *Strategy Formulation: Analytical Concepts*. St. Paul, MN: West Publishing Company, p. p. 85.

10.   Hofer, C.W. and Schendel, D. (1978). *Strategy Formulation: Analytical Concepts*. St. Paul, MN: West Publishing Company, p. p. 160.

11.   Goodstein, Leonard D., Nolan, Timothy M. and Pfeiffer, J. William (1993). *Applied Strategic Planning: A Comprehensive Guide*. New York: McGraw-Hill, p. 240.

12.   Rue, L. and Holland, P. (1986). *Strategic Management*. New York: McGraw-Hill, p. 488.

13.   Hofer, C.W. and Schendel, D. (1978). *Strategy Formulation: Analytical Concepts*. St. Paul, MN: West Publishing Company, p. p. 160, p. 33 and pp. 71–72.

14.   Rue, L. and Holland, P. (1986). *Strategic Management*. New York: McGraw-Hill, p. 238–40.

15.   Schendel, D.E. and Hofer, C.W.(eds.) (1979). *Strategic Management – A New View of Business Policy and Planning*. Boston: Little, Brown, p. 206.

16.   Chang, Y.N. and Campo-Flores, Fileman (1980). *Business Policy and Strategy: Texts and Cases*. Santa Monica, CA: Goodyear Publishing Company, Inc.

17.   Glueck, William F. and Jauch, Lawrence R. (1984). *Business Policy and Strategic Management*. New York: McGraw-Hill Book Company.

18.   Sharplin, Arthur (1985). *Strategic Management*. New York: McGraw-Hill Book Company.

19.   Wheelen, Thomas L. and Hunger, David J. (1992). *Strategic Management and Business Policy* (fourth edition). Reading, MA: Addison-Wesley.

20.   Hofer, C.W. and Schendel, D. (1978). *Strategy Formulation: Analytical Concepts*. St. Paul, MN: West Publishing Company, pp. 123–39.

21.   Rue, L. and Holland, P. (1986). *Strategic Management*. New York: McGraw-Hill, p. 495.

22.   Hofer, Charles W. (1980). 'Turnaround strategies,' *The Journal of Business Strategy*, Vol. 1, No. 1.

Chapter 6

1.   Osell, Roger R. and Wright, Robert V.L. (1980). 'Allocating resources: How to do it in multi-industry corporations,' Chapter 8 in Kenneth J. Albert (ed.) *Handbook of Business Problem Solving*. New York: McGraw-Hill.

2.   Johnson, Gerry and Scholes, Kevan (1993). *Exploring Corporate Strategy: Text and Cases* (third edition). New York: Prentice-Hall, pp. 250–54.

3.   Johnson, Gerry and Scholes, Kevan (1993). *Exploring Corporate Strategy: Text and Cases* (third edition). New York: Prentice-Hall, p. 251.

4.   Hax, Arnoldo C. and Majluf, Nicolas S. (1984). *Strategic Management: An Integrative Perspective*. Englewood Cliffs, NJ: Prentice-Hall, p. 183.

5.   Osell, Roger R. and Wright, Robert V.L. (1980). 'Allocating resources: How to do it in multi-industry corporations,' Chapter 8 in Kenneth J. Albert (ed.) *Handbook of Business Problem Solving*. New York: McGraw-Hill.

6. Hax, Arnoldo C. and Majluf, Nicolas S. (1984). *Strategic Management: An Integrative Perspective.* Englewood Cliffs, NJ: Prentice-Hall, p. 192.

7. Patel, Peter and Younger, Michael (1978). 'A frame of reference for strategic development,' *Long Range Planning*, Vol. 11 (April), pp. 6–12.

8. Patel, Peter and Younger, Michael (1978). 'A frame of reference for strategic development,' *Long Range Planning*, Vol. 11 (April), p. 8.

9. Hax, Arnoldo C. and Majluf, Nicolas S. (1984). *Strategic Management: An Integrative Perspective.* Englewood Cliffs, NJ: Prentice-Hall, pp. 190–1.

10. Younger, Michael (1984). 'Assessing opportunities for diversification – an analytical approach,' *Long Range Planning*, Vol. 17, No. 4, pp. 10–14.

11. Hax, Arnoldo C. and Majluf, Nicolas S. (1984). *Strategic Management: An Integrative Perspective.* Englewood Cliffs, NJ: Prentice-Hall, p. 201.

12. Porter, M.E. (1980). *Competitive Strategy: Techniques for Analysing Industries and Competitors.* New York: Free Press.

13. Patel, Peter and Younger, Michael (1978). 'A frame of reference for strategic development,' *Long Range Planning*, Vol. 11 (April), pp. 6–12.

14. Osell, Roger R. and Wright, Robert V.L. (1980). 'Allocating resources: How to do it in multi-industry corporations,' Chapter 8 in Kenneth J. Albert (ed.) *Handbook of Business Problem Solving.* New York: McGraw-Hill.

15. Younger, Michael (1984). 'Assessing opportunities for diversification – an analytical approach,' *Long Range Planning*, Vol. 17, No. 4, pp. 10–14.

Chapter 7

1. Chang, Y.N. and Campo-Flores, Fileman (1980). *Business Policy and Strategy*: Texts and Cases. Santa Monica, CA: Goodyear Publishing Company, Inc.

2. Drucker, P.F. (1974). 'The manager and management sciences,' in *Management: Task Responsibilities and Practices.* New York: Harper and Row.

3.   Hertz, D.B. and Thomas, H. (1984). *Practical Risk Analysis, An Approach through Case Histories*. Chichester: J. Wiley.

4.   Fisher, G.H. (1971). *Cost Considerations in Systems Analysis*. New York: American Elsevier.

5.   Hertz, David B. (1964). 'Risk analysis in capital investment,' *Harvard Business Review*, Vol. 42 (January–February), pp. 95–106.

6.   Robey, Daniel (1991). *Designing Organizations* (third edition). Homewood, IL: Irwin, p. 292.

7.   Harvey, Donald F. (1982). *Business Policy and Strategic Management*. Columbus OH: Charles Merril Publishing.

8.   Byars, Lloyd L. (1991). *Strategic Management – Formulation and Implementation – Concepts and Cases* (third edition). New York: HarperCollins.

9.   Hosmer, La Rue T. (1982). *Strategic Management – Text Cases on Business Policy*. Englewood Cliff, NJ: Prentice-Hall, p. 315.

10.   Hofer, C.W. and Schendel, D. (1978). *Strategy Formulation: Analytical Concepts*. St. Paul, MN: West Publishing Company, p. 84.

11.   Porter, M.E. (1980). *Competitive Strategy: Techniques for Analysing Industries and Competitors*. New York: Free Press, p. xix.

12.   Byars, Lloyd L. (1991). *Strategic Management – Formulation and Implementation – Concepts and Cases* (third edition). New York: HarperCollins.

13.   Hussey, David E. (1978). 'Portfolio analysis: Practical experience with the directional policy matrix,' *Long Range Planning*, Vol. 11 (August), pp. 2–8.

14.   Adam, Everette E. Jr. and Ebert, Ronald J. (1978). *Production and Operations Management*. Englewood Cliffs, NJ: Prentice-Hall, pp. 453–5.

Chapter 8

1.   Cardozo, Richard N. and Wind, Jerry (1985). 'Risk return approach to product portfolio strategy,' *Long Range Planning*, Vol. 18 (April), pp. 77–85.

2.   Hertz, David B. (1964). 'Risk analysis in capital investment,' *Harvard Business Review*, Vol. 42 (January–February), pp. 95–106.

3.   Markowitz, H.M. (1959). *Portfolio Selection: Efficient Diversification of Investments*. New York: J. Wiley.

4.   Urban, Glen L. and Hauser, John R. (1980). *Designing and Marketing of New Products*. Englewood Cliffs, NJ: Prentice-Hall.

5.   Green, Paul E. and Wind, Yoram (1975). 'New way to measure consumers' judgement,' *Harvard Business Review*, Vol. 53 (July–August), pp. 107–17.

6.   Wind, Yoram and Mahajan, Vijay (1981). 'Designing product and business portfolios,' *Harvard Business Review*, Vol. 59 (January–February), pp. 155–65.

7.   Derkinderen, Frans G.J. and Crum, Roy L. (1984). 'Pitfalls in using portfolio techniques: Assessing risk and potential,' *Long Range planning*, Vol. 19 (April), pp. 129–36.

8.   Brauers, W.K. (1986). 'Essay review article: Risk, uncertainty and risk analysis,' *Long Range Planning*, Vol. 19, pp. 139–43

9.   Hertz, D.B. and Thomas, H. (1984). *Practical Risk Analysis, An Approach through Case Histories*. Chichester: J. Wiley.

Chapter 9

1.   Wind, Yoram and Mahajan, Vijay (1981). 'Designing product and business portfolios,' *Harvard Business Review*, Vol. 59 (January–February), pp. 155–65.

2.   Hussey, David E. (1978). 'Portfolio analysis: Practical experience with the directional policy matrix,' *Long Range Planning*, Vol. 11 (August), pp. 2–8.

Index

183

Authors' index